1982

MAKING SUCCESS
A HABIT

by Steve Musseau

Foreword by Astronaut James B. Irwin

Follow these guides, add a little
common sense, and you will
approach problems the winning way

pluribus
press

CHICAGO 1982

Library of Congress Catalog Card Number:
81-85812

International Standard Book Number:
0-931028-24-8 (Paperbound)
0-931028-26-4 (Clothbound)

Pluribus Press, Division of Teach 'em, Inc.
160 East Illinois Street
Chicago, Illinois 60611

Printed in the United States of America

To My Beloved Spouse Yolanda

Table of Contents

Foreword

What do you do after you have been to the moon? Is there anything else to equal that? Many have asked, "What should I do with my life now?" Some have had severe problems as they grasped for a new goal. My goals were always very easy to visualize. For many years I lived to fly the fastest and highest flying jet aircraft. Then I progressed to flying spacecraft, and a new goal emerged. Our president set the goal for the country, but it seemed like it was set just for me. President Kennedy said, "We will go to the moon in this decade and safely return to the earth. We shall do this not because it is easy but because it is hard. This goal will serve to organize and measure the best of our energies and skills." It is great when you can see your goal so clearly. I gave myself totally to this project. You quickly get caught up with the spirit of adventure and exploration. There were thousands of highly motivated, talented people also rushing toward this goal. I have always been a highly motivated person. I knew that if I was to succeed that I must work hard.

Now ten years have passed since I reached my lifetime goal. Since that time I have come to realize that there are many people who do not have goals and are not motivated. They are looking for success but do not know how to proceed. The purpose of this book is to help people find a plan to greater satisfaction with life.

I met Steve Musseau several years ago. My wife and I attended one of his seminars, and we decided our children could also benefit from such a course. I was delighted to learn that Steve had incorporated all his ideas into a book. I was more delighted to learn that I could write an endorsement or foreword for this book.

Steve is a super motivator. He was a successful coach for several years. To be a successful coach, you have to be able to motivate. He has motivated all our family with his seminars. His practical illustrations are very graphic and not forgotten. This is a positive approach that will enable you to visualize your dreams and then achieve that dream. The approach works. Keep the book handy so you can review it. See if your life doesn't take on a new zest as you discover what you can do.

Plutarch said, "The mind is not a vessel to be filled, but a fire to be lighted." Steve's book will hopefully kindle the flame of your spirit.

Colonel James B. Irwin,
Apollo XV Astronaut,
Colorado Springs, CO
January 1982

Introduction

Last summer we had the world's championship rodeo here in Colorado Springs. I spent several days at the rodeo walking around the grounds and observing the people. I enjoy doing that. One afternoon while strolling around the grounds, I saw a balloon salesman. He was by far the most prominent person at the rodeo. He had about 30 or 40 balloons; every size, shape and color that one could imagine. It made a beautiful bouquet. As I observed this balloon salesman I noticed that most of the children were also attracted to him. They would come up and ask the balloon salesman for that skinny white balloon and the salesman would reach up for the string just under the balloon and would trace it down to his hand and pull it out and give it to the child. Then another child would come up and ask for a fat yellow one and the salesman would follow the same procedure. Occasionally one would escape and float up into the air. Needless to say, this proved to be very frustrating to the salesman because he was losing his profits. As I was observing this I could really identify with his frustration and I began to chuckle to myself. While standing and observing this activity and chuckling to myself, I noticed a small boy standing next to me. He also began to chuckle as he observed this scene. After a while the little boy went up to the balloon salesman and began to tug on his arm. The balloon salesman looked at the little boy and asked him, "What do you want?" and the boy asked the balloon salesman: "Mister, if you let one of those fat red balloons go, would it go up like the rest of them?" The balloon salesman with all of the wisdom in the world looked at the boy and said, "Little boy, it's not the size or the shape or the color of the balloon that makes it go up, but rather, it's what's on the inside."

Now that's what this book is about. We will not talk about sizes or shapes or colors, but rather, we are going to talk about what's on the inside. What's on the inside of each individual person and what's on the inside of each facility because that's what makes any person or organization go up (succeed).

If we are, with any degree of consistency, going to move toward our goals and become goal achievers it is absolutely essential that we internalize our goals, both individually and corporately.

Many years ago during the height of the Depression there was an old Indian living on a reservation in Oklahoma. This old Indian was very poor just like all of the others on the reservation. One day they struck oil on the reservation and the old Indian was very proud of his new wealth. He wanted the whole world to know how wealthy he was. In those days wealthy people drove touring cars. Now a touring car was a sedan convertible. On the back of the car was a trunk and on the back of the trunk were two spare tires. The real wealthy people used to order these touring cars with four spare tires on the back. When you saw someone driving a touring car with four spare tires you knew that the person who owned this car was super rich. So the old Indian ordered a touring car — but he ordered one with six spare tires. He wanted people to know, without a shadow of a doubt, that he was super rich. Not only that but he also chose to get in his car during the noon hour (the busiest time of day) and drive down the main street of this little, hot, dusty Oklahoma town. He would get so excited that he would let go of the steering wheel and wave to the people. He was even known to stand up in the seat and let go of the steering wheel and wave with both hands. Sometimes he would turn all the way around. In spite of this type of behavior during the busiest time of day, he never had an accident, never did any property damage, never did any bodily harm. The people in town said the reason he never had an accident was because of what he had directly in front of the car. Directly in front of the car were two white horses pulling it. Now the mechanic in that town said there was nothing wrong with the engine. As a matter of fact, there were 150 horses underneath the hood just waiting to be turned on. But no one had ever given him the key and showed him how to turn it on. I believe that most of us, individually and corporately, are similar to that old Indian. We have all kinds of horses just waiting to be turned on but no one has ever given us the key. In the following chapters we are going to provide you with the key to turn it on. From the C.E.O.'s all the way down the ladder.

The information that follows is a total concept on goal setting and goal achievement. It is probably quite different from any goal setting techniques that you have previously been exposed to. It is essential that you walk through the book, chapter by chapter, if you are to get the results that you expect. One chapter (concept) builds upon the other.

Success — What Is It?

As a management consultant and *entertrainer* I frequently speak to groups. As a matter of fact, the greatest demand upon my time over the last eight years has been speaking requests. Throughout my adult life I have probably spoken to almost a million people. In the process of speaking with all of these people I have had the opportunity of sharing and listening to many of them. I can never recall having heard anyone, of all those people, come up to me and say, "Steve, I'm planning my life to fail." Never once have I heard anyone verbalize that phrase. But I have, in fact, met many people who are planning their lives to fail. They just haven't verbalized it. Because you don't have to plan to fail. All you have to do is fail to plan. That guarantees it.

I read some statistics the other day that were frightening. The article I was reading pointed out that most people spend more time planning a two week vacation than they do their lives. The article also observed that there is more planning time involved in a high school football practice than in the life of a family. As I travel throughout the country, consulting and counseling executives, I find that the number one challenge for all executives today is the family. They have spent their time and effort to climb the ladder of success only to find it was *leaning against the wrong wall*. It has been my observation that as long as one was having negative challenges in one area of his or her life it affects all of the other areas. Very much like a car running on only three good tires with the fourth being flat.

Or running on only three cylinders when the car has four. Please remember the information in this book is intended to be used in all areas of your life. You are more than a person who administers to an institution or firm.

I frequently ask people, "Do you want or plan to fail?" Obviously the answer is "No." Then I ask, "Do you want or plan to succeed?" The answer is "Yes." But when I ask, "What is success to you?" a look of absolute astonishment often is the reply. Usually I get an, "I don't know," or if I do get an answer it will frequently have something to do with money or materialistic ideas. Now don't misunderstand me; there is nothing wrong with money or material desires. It's just that I don't think that either has anything to do with success.

So that we can begin on common ground, let's share three definitions of success.

I. Whatever makes one feel happy and fulfilled

Based on my awareness, if I am doing something that causes me to feel happy and fulfilled, I am a success. In that same article that I read about time spent planning and goal setting, I also read where, in the same poll, people were asked if they liked their job. Less than 20 per cent of the people said yes. Now if I don't like what I am doing, how can I ever be successful based upon the above definition? The thing that we are so fouled up on is the term happy. Everyone on the face of the earth wants to be happy and yet we never take the time to define it. We have a saying at United Learning Institute: "If you can define it you can measure it. If you can measure it you can have it. If you can't define or measure it you can't have it." Many of us think that if I get more or better I'll be happy. I enjoy visiting elementary schools and as I visit the first, second and third grades I can't help but notice the happiness and the radiant smiles of the children and yet as I visit the fourth, fifth and sixth grades the mouths seem to turn down more often. That radiance seems to have disappeared. I believe the difference is in discovery. As long as I am in the process of discovery, I am experiencing some degree of happiness. I think that as long as our employees are in the process of discovery they, too, will experience a degree of happiness. It is only when we cease to discover that we become unhappy. I am so thankful that my wife, Yolanda, has kept me in the process of discovery in our marriage. For I fear that once there is nothing left to discover about Yolanda I might get bored and lose my enthusiasm.

Abraham Maslow, in his book, *Motivation and Personality*, mentions the four levels of learning. He describes them as:

1. The unconscious incompetent. It means we are stupid and don't know it.
2. The conscious incompetent. We're stupid and we do know it.
3. The conscious competent. We know how to do it and we understand how we do it.
4. The unconscious competent. We do it so well that we don't have to think about doing it. Like a golf swing, or typing, or walking.

The problem with most employees is that they reach the unconscious competent stage and they cease to discover. Therefore, they become bored and unhappy. One of the elements of motivation is to take a person at the unconscious incompetent stage and manage him so that he works his way through the four stages of learning and then, once again, expose him to new information that causes him, once again, to work his way through the four stages. That way he is continuously in the process of discovery. Somewhere in Maslow's book he mentions that we all have a life line and we all have a purpose line. Between the ages of 21 and 35 we are usually at our peak. Around 35 we begin to deteriorate physically. We are either where we want to be or we know we're going to make it. If our life line meets with our purpose line around age 35 we die. Not necessarily a physical death but rather this is the person that has retired and neglected to tell the administration. Therefore, it is absolutely essential to continue to change the purpose line about every three or four years once we get to 35. This causes us to continue to reach and stretch. We keep growing and discovering.

II. How do you compare with your own best self? (And not anyone else)

There was this man who worked at a factory in this town and every day he would walk to work. On his way to work he passed by the watchmaker's shop and every morning for five years he would stop in front of the watchmaker's shop. A huge clock was in front of it. Each morning this man would spend four to five minutes glancing up at the clock and into his hands. Well after five years the owner of the store, who was the watchmaker, was overcome with curiosity and so he went out and asked the man: "What do you do?" The man replied: "I work at the factory at the end of the street." The watchmaker asked: "What do you do at the factory?" Whereupon the man replied: "I have the most important job at the factory; I blow the whistle. I tell people when to come to work, when to take off for lunch, when to come back and when to go home in the evening. If I blow the whistle at the wrong time 1,500 people might be working overtime and not getting paid for it. I figure that the most accurate clock in town is the clock in front of the watchmaker's store. So I spend several minutes each day making sure that my watch is in agreement with your clock because I want to blow the whistle on time." The watchmaker was astonished and said: "That's incredible. I set this clock every day by the whistle."

This is called *follow the follower* and it leads straight to mediocrity. Don't compare yourself with anyone else. Compare yourself with your own best self and I'm sure you'll compare favorably with anyone.

III. How to move steadily toward predetermined worthwhile goals

Too many people think that they will be successful once they reach the goal. Based upon my awareness, if I have some predetermined, worthwhile goals in my life and each day I move closer to those goals, I'm a success. If I am a better administrator today than I was yesterday, I'm a success. If I'm a better manager today than I was yesterday, I'm a success. If I'm a better provider, a better spouse, a better parent today than I was yesterday, I'm a success. At United Learning Institute we believe that *success is a journey, not a destination.*

We are the Robots of Our Thoughts

We are born with a large blank map in our mind. As we go through life we begin to gather pieces to fill in the blank map; very much like a jigsaw puzzle. We begin to gather data about various kinds of people, about this kind of job, and about that kind of environment. As we gather this data it is stored in our subconscious as "truth." The truth about various kinds of people, that kind of environment or this kind of job. When we encounter information that conflicts with this "truth" it makes us feel very uncomfortable and we push away from this truth. We don't want to accept it.

To illustrate what I mean, I will give you a perception. Check to see how accurately you perceive things. It's very important that we perceive things accurately, because what we perceive we believe to be "reality" and we store it as "reality." Every decision we make will be based on this "reality," this "truth."

Our awareness is the key to our success. We cannot become anything that our awareness does not permit us to become and awareness is defined as: How clearly I perceive and understand everything that affects my life. It is the automatic product of my entire life experiences. So let's see how accurately we perceive things.

Please read the following statement *once*, close the book and write the statement on a piece of paper:

"A bird in the the hand is worthless"----

Now we have been talking about a map in your mind. Let's check your perception about another map with which you are quite familiar. The map of the United States. Please, on that same piece of paper that you wrote down the statement about the bird, write down either true or false for each of the statements that follow:

1) Jacksonville, FL, is southeast of Cleveland.
2) Los Angeles, CA, is southwest of Reno, NV.
3) Montreal, Canada, is northeast of Seattle, WA.

Now on the same piece of paper answer these riddles.

A) How many of each species did Moses take on the ark?
B) What was the name of those tablets that Noah brought down from the mountain?

Check all of your answers once more to make certain that they are correct.

Now, on the first one about the bird, did you have, "A bird in the the hand is worthless?" In other words, did you have two "The's?"

On the next one, "Jacksonville, FL, is southeast of Cleveland, OH." Did you write true? If you did you are wrong. Jacksonville, FL, is southwest of Cleveland, OH.

If you said true to the statement that Los Angeles is southwest of Reno, you are wrong again. Los Angeles is southeast of Reno, NV.

Montreal, Canada, is southeast of Seattle, WA, not northeast.

On the riddle, "How many of each species did Moses bring on the ark?" the answer is *none*. Moses didn't have an ark; it was Noah.

If you listed "The Ten Commandments" to the riddle, "What was the name of those tablets that Noah brought down from the mountain," you were, once again, wrong. It was Moses that brought the tablets down from the mountain. So you see our perceptions are not what we might have thought them to be. And our awareness is how clearly we *perceive* and understand everything that affects our life. We all consider ourselves experts in perception. But as you can see that is not necessarily true.

We don't act, behave or perform in accordance with "truth," but rather, we act, behave and perform in accordance with "truth" as we perceive it. To illustrate the above, would you please read the information that follows, one time:

FINISHED FILES ARE THE
RESULT OF YEARS OF SCIENTIF-
IC STUDY COMBINED WITH THE
EXPERIENCE OF MANY YEARS.

Now that you have read it through one time, count the number of F's. Write the number down on a piece of paper. You might want to count them once again to make sure. How many did you count? Did you count 6 F's? You didn't! Then count them one more time. Now how many did you count? Did you count 6 F's this time? If not maybe you didn't count the F's in the word "of." You will notice the word "of" appears three times.

The reason that you might have missed the F's in the word "of" is because of a process known as a *scotoma*. A scotoma is defined as a sensory locking out of our environment based on prior conditioning and/or expectation. You see, you and I learned to read phonetically and "of" is not "of." We pronounce it "ov." So we were conditioned to see "of" as "ov." We don't see with our eyes; we see with our mind. We only perceive light through our eyes and so since we were conditioned to see "of" as "ov" we lock it out. It's just not there. We have scotomas about our family. What are we locking out about our wife? About our children? We have scotomas about our job. What truths are we locking out about the opportunities of our job?

About 500 years ago there was a sailor here on earth whose name was Christopher Columbus. Now when Columbus lived on this earth most of the people believed it was flat. So how did they behave? They would get into their boats and sail out three or four miles and then turn around and come back. Why? Because they believed that if they would sail out any further they would sail over the edge. Now the earth has never been flat; it's always been a sphere. But the people behaved in accordance with "truth" as they perceived it. And so along comes this crazy guy by the name of Christopher Columbus. He says to his friends sitting in the local pub, "We're going to sail around the world." And they very nervously say, "We, who?" Christopher Columbus must have been one of the greatest leaders the world has ever known. Can you imagine convincing three boat loads of people to sail around a world that they believed was flat? That's what leadership is. Convincing others to believe what you know to be "truth" even though it conflicts with their belief. "Truth" doesn't rule the world but rather imagination rules the world. It's not necessarily the truth that dictates our actions but rather what we imagine to be true.

As we have previously mentioned, the material in this book is an *awareness opportunity*. Most of us pride ourselves on our level of awareness.

We are totally unique individuals. No two of us have the same awareness and thus the same values, needs or desires.

If I am functioning on a limited or distorted awareness, then my actions and decisions will be both limited and distorted. Example: Our first year in administration we did the very best job possible based upon our awareness at that time. But our awareness changed and increased; therefore, our actions and decisions as administrators gained greater depth.

Awareness is how clearly I perceive and understand everything that affects my life. It is the automatic product of my entire life experience. Although my awareness is in a continual state of flux at the moment of any decision it is absolutely fixed. In other words, at that moment it is where my awareness was; therefore, it was the only decision I could have made. That is why it is so important that we are perceiving things as they really are so that our awareness might be more "right on."

We can never be fully aware of what is going on around us

because we would go crazy. As you are reading this book there are all kinds of things going on around you that you are not aware of. For example: The pressure of the watch on your wrist, the ring on your finger, your collar, your belt or the noise of the heating system or perhaps birds singing. Every hair on your body is continually sending information to your brain. Perhaps you have wondered why some people seem to be more aware than others or why some people seem to see more new opportunities than others. Why are some people more open to new ideas and innovations in administration? It is because of the many limiting factors that influence our awareness. We have many physical limitations. Limitations in our sight, our perception, and consequently, our awareness is corrected through the use of glasses, microscopes and telescopes, and so forth. Our hearing is limited when we compare our range of hearing with dogs, bats or porpoises. Our sense of smell is minor compared to bloodhounds or the male silk moth who is capable of smelling a female moth seven miles away. Therefore, it is easy to see that our senses do place limitations on our awareness. So the question is why don't I sense these things that are going on around me? It is because of one of the greatest controlling factors of my awareness: *the reticular activating system.* This is a group of net-like cells at the base of the brain that monitors sensory messages to the brain; a built-in filtering device that allows only personally profitable information to get through (as does a good executive secretary). That which has *pay value.* That which has personal profitability to me.

The only things that get through my filter system are those which have *pay value* to me. What is pay value? Why did I learn to ride a bike? Because my girlfriend moved 10 blocks away. Why did I learn to drive a car? Because my girlfriend moved 10 miles out of town. It had pay value to learn to ride a bike, pay value to learn to drive a car. Here are some examples of how the reticular activating system works. You're walking through an air terminal and there are all kinds of noises and the public address system is blaring. You really don't hear what it is saying but your name comes across the system. Right away you hear it. Your name has pay value to you. A mother sleeps through all kinds of traffic noise but hears the slightest whimper from her baby.

Right now, without looking, vividly describe your watch. What make, what color, face and hands? What kinds of numbers, whether arabic, roman, or just slashes? Now check to see how accurate you are. Right now, turn your watch over. With your watch turned over, what time did it have? It is most important that we understand the concepts of *filter system* and *pay value* so that we can increase our awareness and become goal achievers.

Principles:

1. I must know what I want before I can become aware of how to get it.
2. I determine what has pay value.

When I do these two things, then the filter system *automatically* opens to all relevant and important information.

Examples:

1. I'm in the market for a new house. It's amazing how many houses I see for sale.
2. I'm driving down the freeway. I must know my destination before I can find the correct exit.

I can increase my own awareness of valuable opportunities by making certain that I first know *exactly* what it is I want for my life. Exact house, car, job, vacation, and so forth. Luck is no accident! It's when *preparation* meets *opportunity*. The consistently lucky person is one who knows what he or she is looking for. Knows the *pay value* and opens the filter thereby receiving the information that assists in achieving goals. But *remember*, preconceived ideas (or conditioning) causes us to see what we *expect* to see; hear what we *expect* to hear; find what we *expect* to find. We frequently develop scotomas to the truth.

How does this apply to administration? Frequently correcting and directing the same employee over and over again. Pretty soon you expect him or her to make trouble. You develop a scotoma to the fact that others might be contributing to the problem. There is another concept that also contributes to our distorted awareness. This concept is known as the *L.O. L.O.* concept or the lock on lock out. The *L.O. L.O.* concept makes change difficult. We define the *L.O. L.O.* concept: We develop a sentimental or emotional attachment to those things to which we are exposed to first. We can only consciously see one thing at a time.

Look at the picture above. What do you see? Do you see a hat? A fireplace? An arrow? Or do you see the word "Fly?" Look at the white. You might have great difficulty seeing the word "fly" because you are *locked on* to black figures on a white background. Once you *lock on* it's very difficult to see anything else.

Examples:

We go to the same vacation spot over and over.
Same barber.
Same restaurant.
Same route to and from work.
Same way of administering.

How many of us are *locked on* to doing a super job at work and go home and lock out the family?

How many of us are *locked on* to doing something a particular way and are *locking out* anything new and innovative? *Flexibility* and *creativity* are two very important ingredients to *effectively* deal with change but locking on to something tends to kill both creativity and flexibility. We become narrow, opinionated and unimaginative. We need to lock on and make decisions about job, friends, home, everything in life. We need to scan continually for new information if we expect to grow.

Remember! What was good administrative policy yesterday is no longer accepted as appropriate.

Things are changing and if we expect to stay up with the change it is absolutely essential that we understand the function of setting and achieving meaningful goals.

Sometimes we work overtime to make certain that our awareness remains distorted. Have you noticed that once you have made a decision on something, you find all kinds of ways to support the decision. Example: Getting married to Yolanda.

I had a decision to make. Whether to get married or remain single. Once I made a decision to marry Yolanda I found literally thousands of reasons why this was a good decision. Had I decided to remain single I would have found reasons to support the decision. We are always gathering data to support our decisions and beliefs. This phenomenon is called the *cognitive dissonance theory*. This theory was developed by Leon Festinger.

We cannot support two conflicting beliefs at the same time without causing disharmony. We gather data to support our dominant beliefs. We are perhaps more rationalizing than rational, continually gathering data to prove that our decisions are *not absurd.*

1. I have decided to buy a new automobile. I want a Volvo and my wife wants a Vega. I win and we buy a Volvo. Suddenly I read in the paper where Vegas are being re-

called. I see Vegas broken down on the side of the road but never any Volvos. I read where Volvo is very safe and I make certain that my spouse sees it also.

2. I get in a fight with my wife and I go down to the corner tavern. I tell all of my buddies my version of the fight. They all sympathize and say, "Yeah, they're all alike. I have one just like it. You're right."

Rationalization is not necessarily a bad quality but recognize that it's a tendency that we all have. All too frequently our opinions and beliefs become predictors of our future behavior.

Examples: That employee is not going to make it. (sure enough)

I'm not going to have a good time at the party. (sure enough)

VERSUS

That employee is going to make a positive contribution. (sure enough)

I'm going to have a great time at the party. (sure enough)

The Harvard Test of Reflective Acquisition is another good example. It is generally agreed that students learn in spurts. They go along for a while, settle at plateaus and then suddenly spurt forward in a particular skill or learning activity. The Harvard Test was developed to test an individual's spurt potential; to see if kids could be identified and nurtured at the moment they were about to spurt. Results: Sure enough, those identified by the test as spurters all spurted.

In a subsequent experiment, students were chosen at random, but the teachers were told that they had been identified as spurters. Results: Those who did not spurt got plenty of attention from teachers and spurted anyway because teachers expected them to, based upon the mythical test.

Don't get down on yourself when you don't perform up to capacity. You are doing the best that your current awareness will permit you to do. Remember, our awareness can be expanded and sharpened as we go through life. We promise to share with you some powerful ways to change old habits and attitudes that are causing your limited awareness.

In the Book of Proverbs in the Bible it says, "As a man thinketh in his heart, so is he." Since we are a product of our thoughts it becomes readily apparent that it is essential for us to understand how we think our thought process.

The diagrams that are used in this section are strictly pragmatic. We simply use them as illustrations. The illustrations are not intended to be loci in the brain. As we describe how we think there are three separate parts and each part has its own particular functions.

The three parts of the brain as we describe them are conscious, subconscious and creative subconscious. As we have mentioned each part has its own functions.

Let's first look at the functions of the conscious part of the brain. On the conscious level we perceive our environment through our senses. We all consider ourselves experts in perception. Whatever we perceive, we perceive to be reality and once it is perceived it is stored in our subconscious as "truth" and "reality." We then *associate* each new experience with that "truth." What do I know or what have I seen or experienced that is similar to this? How did I react to that situation? What were the results? We then evaluate it.

How will I be influenced if I do it this way? The last time I experienced a situation similar to this, this is what happened and then, I made this decision. Therefore I will make this decision again. When my son John was young and learning to ride his two wheel bicycle he was going to run into a tree so I ran in front of the bike to stop him. I was successful in this venture. When he was 17 years old and learning to drive an automobile, a similar situation presented itself. John headed the automobile toward a tree. Now it would have been pretty final had I decided to run in front of the car to stop it. So the fourth function of the conscious part of the thought process is to make a decision based upon perception, association, evaluation. This is why it is so very important to sharpen our awareness and begin to perceive things more accurately.

The subconscious part of the thought process has two functions. We have already mentioned one of them. It stores data as "truth" and "reality." Whatever the conscious perceives to be true it stores in the subconscious as "truth." Another function of the subconscious is it handles automatic activities and over-learned skills. Some examples of automatic activities: our respiratory system, our circulatory system, our endocrine system, our digestive system, etc. In other words those functions which require no conscious thoughts on our part. Even though we can be asleep or unconscious they would still continue to function. What about over-learned skills? Walking is an over-learned skill. Have you ever observed infants learning to walk? They are struggling to maintain balance. Every step is a conscious effort. But you don't think to walk, you just walk. Learning to write is also an over-learned skill. First graders learning to write struggle with each letter. It is a conscious effort but after awhile you don't think to write, you just write.

Driving a stick shift is a very good example that you can probably remember if you are old enough. Remember when your dad took you out that Saturday morning on the back roads to teach you how to drive and how nervous you were when he gave you the keys and told you to sit behind the wheel? Then when he told you to put the key in the ignition, you didn't know what he meant. Then your father pointed to the hole where the key wasn't. He then instructed you to turn it on and you did but the automobile was in gear. Your father probably started to scream and told you to put it in neutral. You probably asked some intelligent question like, "What's a neutral?" Your father explained what neutral was and you started the car. He then instructed you to put the car in first. Whereupon you asked, "Well how do I do that?" He told you to pull the shift toward you and down. You did precisely that and you almost ripped the gear box out of its housing. Your father then told you to press on the clutch and of course you didn't know what the clutch was. So you asked and he told you it was one of those pedals. More specifically the far left pedal. You pressed on the clutch, put the gear in first and then your father told you to let out on the clutch. You did this and the car began to buck uncontrollably. Your father had you start over again but this time give it more gas. So you went through the procedure once again but this time you really revved up the engine and let up the clutch and you made skid marks all over the highway. That was a horrible experience. But now you can drive 55 m.p.h., smoke a cigarette, drink a bottle of pop, talk to a friend and wave to neighbors. You can do all kinds of things while driving your car. You have turned it over to your subconscious. Ninety per cent of our daily activities are handled by habits of thought or habits of action. It's a very effective and efficient way of functioning.

The creative subconscious part of our thought process has three distinctive functions. It maintains sanity; it solves and resolves conflict; it reduces stress. It's like a built-in psychotherapist. We are continuously gathering data to prove that the decisions we make are correct. As an example: When we first had a big price hike in gasoline, I was driving a large car that averaged about 11 miles to the gallon. I was also driving about 50,000 miles per year. Well when the price of gasoline doubled I could no longer afford to drive this car. Because I drove so many miles I wanted to drive a comfortable safe car that got good mileage. I decided to purchase a Mercedes diesel. When I found out the price, I figured it was too expensive. As I shopped around I went to a dealer who sold Peugeots. I found that the Peugeot made a diesel and that it was comfortable and safe. So I took my spouse, Yolanda, with me and we went down and purchased the car. On the way home I began to ask myself some questions like: "Am I the only person who drives a Peugeot? I don't think I've even heard of a Peugeot before.

Why did I allow that salesman to talk me into purchasing it?" With that kind of thinking one would soon go crazy. My wife was sitting beside me and she is not saying a thing. But I know what she was thinking. "He blew it again." I lived 11 miles from the place where I purchased the vehicle. On the way home I counted 13 Peugeots and of course I pointed them out to my wife while reminding her: "We can't be too crazy, you see many people drive Peugeots." I was gathering data to prove that the decision that I had made was correct. It's part of the cognitive dissonance theory by Leon Festinger that we mentioned earlier.

My creative subconscious "makes me act like me." It selects the most currently dominant image of reality about me and makes me act like that image of reality. For example, suppose my currently dominant image of me is that I do poorly when standing before groups. My creative subconscious will cause me to stutter, stammer and be very nervous while standing before the group. It's very obvious that I can speak because on a one on one I speak very fluently and am very relaxed. If, while under hypnosis, I am told that a ball point pen weighs 300 pounds, I will accept this as "truth." I will not be able to pick up this ball point pen even though my biceps are exerting 100 pounds of energy. The reason for this is my creative subconscious would cause my triceps to exert a counter force of 100 pounds. The creative subconscious doesn't care if I am working up to my potential. It makes me act like my reality. In other words whatever we accept as truth about ourself or about our job, or those kinds of people or whatever, our creative subconscious will work to make it so. As an example: For many years, approximately 20, all of the experts said it was biologically impossible for man to high jump seven feet. We all accepted that as "truth" and no one did. A young man by the name of Charles Dumas jumped seven feet and now high school sophomores are doing it.

This relates to creative problem solving. Having worked for

days on a particular problem, perhaps a financial problem, or a supervisory problem, or a communication problem, you finally decide that you can't arrive at a solution. So you put it aside. Maybe that very night or a week later you wake up in the middle of the night with the solution. But if you go back to sleep and don't record that data right then you probably will not remember the solution in the morning. Get in the habit of recording those creative insights at that very moment.

Get in the habit of recording all of your creative insights even though they seem to have no meaning. Record them in a journal and periodically refer to the journal. In time these ideas will begin to synapse and creatively form new ideas.

Let's suppose you are churning butter. As you churn a yellow hunk appears so you get a fork and fish it out and throw it away. As you continue to churn more yellow chunks appear and you throw them out. Now this is ridiculous. You are throwing away the butter. If you leave the yellow hunks in while you churn they begin to coagulate and form the butter. That's the way that our creative insights work. So don't throw them away; record them in your journal and periodically refer to your journal to see what the picture is beginning to look like. Many of us tend to avoid challenges and as a consequence do not grow. Get in the habit of giving your creative subconscious interesting challenges to solve. This is how we become growth oriented and successful. Get in the habit of dwelling, for a short time, on a challenge. Allow the creative subconscious to percolate the information and creatively figure out a solution. Be ready to write down the solution or put it on a cassette tape.

We must provide drive and energy to do that which we say we are going to do.

Any time my creative subconscious detects an obstacle or challenge that is keeping me from my goals it then provides me with energy and drive to overcome the obstacles and challenges and continue toward my goals. Our natural state is harmony. Therefore if we are faced with a challenge that creates disharmony, we work toward harmony. As an example: Suppose I would call you and your wife tonight and tell you that you had just won a two-week vacation, all expenses paid, to Acapulco but you must leave tomorrow noon. Your creative subconscious would become very active in resolving all obstacles and your reticular activating system, which we mentioned earlier, would be wide open for information. You would creatively find someone to watch the kids, and watch the house, and take care of any details at the office. You would have great drive and energy until your goal had been achieved. Any time the picture of reality that I have in my mind conflicts with the picture of what is, it creates a disparity. My creative subconscious works to resolve the disparity. For example: Name the figures below:

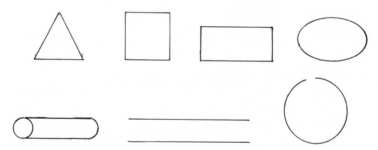

If you named the first a triangle you are correct.
If you named the second a square you are correct.
If you named the third a rectangle you are correct.
If you named the fourth an oval you are correct.
If you named the fifth a cylinder you are correct.
If you named the sixth two parallel lines you are correct.
If you named the seventh a circle you are wrong.

That's correct; you are wrong. It is not a circle. It is an incomplete circle. But you see there was a conflict between what our picture in our mind was and what actually was. Therefore, we corrected it to agree with what we believed to

-25-

be true. This is one of the keys to motivation. We create intentionally a disparity between the picture in our minds with the picture of "what is." We must change "what is" or we will go crazy. In the remaining chapters of this book we will go into much greater detail and explore why and how our attitudes and self-image hold us back.

For example: Why does
— a bowler who averages 150 bowl 190 one game and creatively bowl 110 the next game?
— a golfer who consistently shoots in the low 90's go out and shoot a 40 on the front 9 and a 55 on the back 9?
— a salesperson make $3,000 one month and $1,000 the next?

Why do we, as administrators, start each year saying:
"This year it's going to be different!
I'm going to make good use of my time for planning.
I'm going to have better control of my time.
I'm going to have a more open line of communication."
Why don't we perform the way we want?

Are there some techniques that would enable me to get more of the qualities I want out of life?

We will find out in the next few chapters.

Attitudes and Self-Image — Thermometers or Thermostats?

Let's briefly review how we think.

PERCEIVE **Conscious** DECIDE

ASSOCIATE
EVALUATE

Sub Conscious	Creative Subconscious
1. — Stores Data as Truth and Reality	1. — Maintains Reality Makes Me Act Like Me
2. — Handles Automatic Activities and Overlearned Skills	2. — Creatively Solves Problems
	3. — Provides Drive and Energy

I. **Conscious Process**
    A. Perceives through my senses (reality).
    B. Associates with what's stored in subconscious.
    C. Evaluates (right, wrong, good, bad, etc.)
    D. Makes a decision. (I like it, I don't like it; I'll buy it, I won't buy it, I don't know, I'll wait and see.)

II. **Subconscious (Stores My Reality)**
    Like a computer it stores my version of truth and reality.

As we have already observed our version of reality often is *inaccurate* or *distorted*.

Why? Because of *Garbage In* our subconscious does not question, evaluate, or sort information. It simply accepts everything that our conscious allows to be programmed into it. It is much like a computer. If one programs into a computer $2 \times 2 = 5$ then they will get out of that computer $2 \times 2 = 5$. The same is true of the brain. Whatever we program into it that's what we get out of it. This process is referred to as *G.I.G.O.* Good Stuff In equals Good Stuff Out. Garbage In equals Garbage Out.

To the degree that our image of "truth and reality" is founded on misinformation then our corresponding behavior or actions will also be unwise or inaccurate.

Think back on some of the examples of conditioning, the card with the six F's. But let's say you only perceived three F's (Garbage In). Then the answer you gave was three F's (Garbage Out). Another example of Garbage In Garbage Out: A young boy comes home from school and he tells his father he is having trouble with his math. The father then says, "You come by that quite naturally, son. I was never any good at that stuff either." The boy grows up thinking that he's a carrier. Or the person that says well he's Irish and you know how Irish are. Or I'm Italian and you know how Italians are. These are all Garbage In ideas. Simply because my father was not good at math does not mean that I must also be no good at it, or just because I'm Irish or Italian does not mean that I must behave in a certain way, or just because I was born at a certain time doesn't mean that I must act in a certain way.

III. Creative Subconscious (Maintains My Reality)

A. Makes me act like the picture of me in my subconscious.

B. Solves problems. Very much like a secretary scanning the files for information.
C. Gives me drive and energy to move toward my goal and overcome obstacles.

Our creative subconscious can work *for* or *against* us. For example: If I see myself as a loser even though I am winning I will creatively make sure I lose and vice versa. Remember the example of the ball point pen. If we believe on the subconscious level that the pen weighs 300 pounds we can't pick it up. We know that we can't pick up three hundred pounds so we will creatively make sure that we don't. It's the bicep-tricep concept.

Our creative subconscious does not care whether or not we are acting in our own best interest. It works to fulfill whatever our subconscious picture dictates — regardless of our true potential.

Remember the L.O.L.O. principle: "We develop a sentimental, emotional attachment to that which we are exposed to first." It becomes very difficult to change. A 40-year-old man still spells Febuary rather than February. Once we *lock on* it becomes hard to change because we *lock out* the true answers and true spelling. If I store incorrect information in my subconscious today it will affect my perception image and actions from now on.

We have been alluding to potential and effectiveness. So that you will understand what we mean when we use these terms, let's define them.

Potential is the total capacity that exists within us. There is very little that we can do about potential. It's God's gift to us.

Effectiveness is the degree to which we use our potential. We can alter our effectiveness. We have control over our effectiveness. It's what we do with what we have. It's our gift to God.

Some people that I have had the pleasure of knowing have

come very close to their potential.

1. Peter Strudwick — Peter is a marathon runner. Pete has no feet.

2. Franklin Jacobs — Franklin is a high jumper. A world class high jumper. Franklin high jumps 7' 7¾". Franklin is only 5'8" tall. He jumps almost two feet above his height. The experts will tell you it can't be done. Fortunately they didn't tell Franklin.

3. Helen Keller — deaf, dumb, and blind. But she inspired the world by overcoming her handicaps.

4. Cris Cole — an outstanding blind judge in Houston, Texas.

These people and many many more have performed with excellence in spite of physical handicaps.

Some of us see problems in every opportunity while others see opportunities in every problem.

W. Clement Stone has said: "For every adversity there is a seed of equal or greater benefit."

But we need to look for the seed, plant it, fertilize it, water it and have faith. We don't keep digging it up to see if it is growing.

We want to be certain that we plant good, positive seeds. If we plant a bean we don't get wheat. If we plant wheat we don't get a bean. If we plant a bean we don't get a bean. That's right, we get many beans. Because between planting and harvest multiplication takes place. The same is true with thoughts. If I plant a negative thought I don't get a positive thought and if I plant a negative thought I don't get a negative thought. I get many negative thoughts because between planting and harvest the imagination takes hold. It grows and grows and grows. But turn that around. Plant a positive thought and see what happens. Sometimes the seed we plant might be like the Chinese bamboo tree. The first year we plant it and water it. The second year we fertilize it; the third year the same thing. The fourth year the same thing. The fifth year the same thing and in five weeks it grows 76 feet.

How about administrators?

You have all overcome adversity:
— Long hours of preparation
— Volunteer activities and long hours at work
— Relationship problems with employees.

Certainly we don't need adversities to stimulate our daily achievements. What is it that keeps some administrators from taking off? What holds us back? Do we have to lose our feet, our sight, our hearing before we can come close to our potential?

Ancient Chinese women used to limit the size of their feet by keeping them bound tightly from childhood. Many of us are limited today because of what we accepted in childhood. We, too, have wraps on.

A man won a prize at the county fair for a full grown pumpkin shaped just like a small jug. How did he accomplish this? When the pumpkin started to bloom he simply thrust the bloom into the glass jug and the pumpkin filled the jug. He simply broke the jug and the pumpkin had duplicated the size and shape of the glass jug. Many times we do the same to ourselves. We place ourselves in containers that limit our growth. The container will be just as large or small as we believe it to be. It is a matter of choice. We can choose to continue to grow or we can choose to become ripe and rot. Many times the achievement of our potential is just a matter of a very slight edge, but we don't realize it. For example in baseball a .350 hitter earns at least $250,000 per year. But a .250 hitter may earn $40,000 a year. Yet the difference is only one hit every 10 times at bat. A very slight edge.

How many Super Bowls are won or lost because the team missed a first down by one inch, a pass caught or missed by one inch, a field goal or extra point missed by one inch?

I read an article several years ago on "value." It pointed out that if you took an ingot of iron the value would be $5.00;

however, if you chose to make horseshoes out of this ingot the value would then be $10.50; if you chose to make sewing machine needles out of that ingot of iron the value would then be $4285.00; if you chose to make balance wheels for watches out of that ingot of iron the value would be $250,000.00. So it isn't the raw material that determines the value but rather the processing. This is true of your life and mine. It isn't the raw material that determines our value but rather it is the processing involved. Since this be true, whom do you choose to be the quality controller of your life? I'm certain that *you* choose to be the quality controller of *your* life. This being true, you and I need some tools so that we can become the very best quality controller.

That's what this book is all about.

When I was a young lad one of the happiest days of the year was the day the circus came to town. I was born and reared during the Depression. There were no TV's, very few radios, and we didn't have enough money to go to the movies, which were silent. But mom and dad always managed to save enough so that they could take us to the circus. We used to wake up early and go to the train depot and watch them unload. I was always attracted to the elephants, because they were so big and powerful. They used to push five and six huge wagons around as if they were nothing. Then that evening when we went to the circus we were directed through a tent where they housed the animals. All of the animals were in cages except the camels and the elephants. The only thing separating you from the elephants was a rope. I used to ask my father to take us to the elephants. I would put a peanut in the palm of my hand and offer it to the elephant. When he would take it I would put another one in my hand and offer it to the elephant. But this time I would back up a little. I would continue to play this game with the elephant until I had backed up far enough so that I was several inches beyond his reach. As a little lad this gave me a feeling of great power. To think that such a little fellow like me could hold something in his hand that such a magnificent beast wanted so bad but couldn't reach. I would play this game with the elephants until one day I saw something that frightened me beyond belief. This is what I saw. I saw a mommy elephant and a baby elephant stand next to one another. The baby elephant was tethered by a large chain around her ankle attached to a steel peg driven several feet in the ground. The mommy elephant was tethered by a rope around her ankle and the rope was attached to a wooden peg driven in the ground. I looked at this and thought: "My gosh! They've got them hooked up wrong." But you see they didn't have them hooked up wrong. When the mommy elephant was a baby they hooked her up with the steel chain and steel peg. When she pulled the chain tightened around her ankle. She soon learned that it made no difference how hard or in which direction she pulled, she could go no further. She then quit trying. She had been conditioned. When it pulled tight around her ankle it was foolish to keep trying. They then took off the steel and put on the rope.

How many of us have been conditioned so that we no longer try? It is our opinion that most limitations are self-imposed.

Another example of how, because of conditioning and belief, we put limitations on ourselves. In 1954 track experts said that it was biologically impossible for man to run the mile in less than four minutes. As these experts said this we all nodded our heads and as we did you could hear the rocks roll around. In 1954 a man by the name of Dr. Roger Bannister said: "That's ridiculous, man can run the mile in less than four minutes." Doctor Bannister trained and ran the mile in 3 minutes 59 seconds and 7 tenths. Within that same year 42 other people did it. Now high school sophomores are doing it. But because the "experts" said it could not be done (garbage in) we accepted it as truth and imposed another limitation on ourselves.

As I am writing this I am watching the astronauts. Young and

Crippen have just touched the wheels of the Columbia to the desert floor in California. Twenty years ago if you had told someone that this event would occur at this time they would have had you committed to a mental institution. The "experts" would have said that it was impossible. So let's look at some of the limiting factors that many of us have experienced. Let us begin by discussing attitudes and self-image — "the achievement regulators." Most of us go through life believing that we are thermometers rather than thermostats. We think that we were created to register the environment rather than control it.

As I was listening to the two astronauts, Young and Crippen, communicate with base station, Houston, I heard one of the astronauts mention something about the "attitude" of the spaceship. It was difficult for me to understand what was meant by the "attitude" of a spaceship. A friend of mine was visiting me the next day and I asked him what was meant by the "attitude" of the spaceship. He held out his two arms horizontal to the ground and began to lean in first one direction and then the other. He said: "Imagine that my arms are the wings of an airplane; now as they lean in one direction or the other the plane is said to have an attitude. In other words an attitude is the direction in which I lean."

So very simplistically an attitude is the direction in which we lean either toward something or away from something. If I lean toward something I am said to have a positive attitude! If I lean away from something I am said to have a negative attitude. Therefore, there is no such thing as.a positive or negative attitude in and of itself. An attitude does not become negative or positive until we set a goal. If my attitude leans toward my goal I am said to have a positive attitude. If my attitude leans away from my goal I am said to have a negative attitude. For example, I set a health goal to weigh a less amount, to have a lower cholesterol count, to lower my triglyceride count, to lower my diastolic and systolic blood pressure. If I begin to eat no red meat, limit my dairy products, eggs, and if I begin to limit my salt intake and eliminate processed foods and begin an exercise program that would keep my heart rate up to its "training heart rate" for 35 minutes a day five days a week — then I am leaning toward that goal. I am said to have a positive attitude as far as that goal is concerned. However, if I continue to eat the same kinds of foods in the same proportions and I continue the same life style without any planned exercise, then I'm said to have a negative attitude. Most of us want to change our goals because we are not leaning toward them. We are leaning away from them. The goals don't need changing; the goals are good. The attitudes need changing. So you say, "How do we change attitudes?" Let's first examine how attitudes are formed.

An attitude is a habit of thought, the direction in which we lean either toward or away from something on the subconscious level. Attitudes are formed by three-dimensional self-talk *words* which trigger *pictures* which bring about *feelings*. So we think in three dimensions — words, pictures, feelings. When we were born we did not have an attitude about anything but almost immediately we began to develop attitudes. For example the first day of birth our pants are wet. We cry. Someone changes my diaper. That *feels* so good. I have developed an attitude about wet diapers and dry diapers. My stomach hurts; I cry. Someone feeds me. That *feels* so good. I have developed an attitude about empty stomachs and full stomachs. These attitudes are formed by *feelings*. I have no words. As a matter of fact I have no pictures. There is a membrane over my eyes. So our most fundamental primordial attitudes are formed by *feelings*. Several days after birth someone is caressing me, nurturing me, feeding me and I am really enjoying this *feeling*. The membrane is dissolved from my eyes and I look up to see a picture — probably my mother. I now have an association. A picture with a feeling. I see the picture (mother) and I feel good. I associate the picture with the feeling. I still have no words but when I begin to crawl and pull the ash trays off the table and pull the lamps down, there is a word added to the process. The word is "no." I pull the ash tray off of the table. My mother says, "No." I see she is angry (picture). She spanks my hand (feeling). From that moment on words become a very important part of attitude formation.

Some attitudes are formed by society's opinions. For example it's now OK for women to wear jeans, sweat shirts, and tennis shoes. This used to be considered men's clothing. But you would never see a man in a woman's skirt and blouse. Why? Because society has said it's OK for women to dress as men do but it's not acceptable for men to dress as women.

1. We are born neutral.

2. We begin to interact with the environment.

3. "Experts" evaluate our every performance.

4. Negative and positive thoughts and feelings are deposited (like rocks) on their respective sides of their attitudinal balanced scale.

Attitudinal
Balance
Scale

5. The rocks accumulate and we lean in one direction or another (toward + or away −).

6. An attitude is now formed.

For example: A young boy, age 2½ years old. His mother buys him a coloring book with a box of crayolas and instructs him to take it to his room and learn to paint. He opens the coloring book and the crayolas and is astonished by the rainbow of colors. He takes out a red crayon and marks in the book. Then a blue, a green, a yellow, an orange, and he has made a creation. He wants to share this creation with someone he loves. So he finds his five-year-old sister who is busy playing house with her friend. The 2½ year old boy asks his sister (a real authority in his life and twice as old as he is) what she thinks of the picture. She tells him it is the most stupid painting she has ever seen. She has just taken a large rock and placed it on the negative side of his attitudinal balance scale. Every time he walks by the refrigerator and sees his five-year-old sister's art he is reminded of how stupid he is. Through his own self-talk he piles more negative rocks on the negative side of his attitudinal scale. Several months later when he is three he learns how to stay inside the lines. He wants, once again, to share his painting with someone he loves, but not his five-year-old sister. He looks around the house and finds his nine-year-old brother Tommy. Now, Tommy is a real authority. He is *three* times as old and the little boy loves him very much. But Tommy is playing with some of his friends and doesn't want to be bothered by his three-year-old brother. But his little brother pleads with him to look at this painting. So his brother makes fun of his painting and tells him it's a dumb painting. The little brother informs him, "But I stayed inside the lines." Whereupon his brother Tommy says, "Whoever heard of a cowboy with a green face and a purple horse?"

At age four he is at home and it is raining. His mother is having a party at her home that evening. She is a working mother and hasn't cleaned the house as well as she would like to, so she tells the little boy to go up to his room and paint. Later, that afternoon the mother is vacuuming the carpet. She is running late. She hasn't cooked dinner yet so she is anxious to finish. The little boy comes down from his room, stands in front of the vacuum, and tells his mother to come up to the room to see his painting. But his mother pleads with him several times to move out of the way so that she can finish. But the little boy insists that his mother come to his room and see the painting. Finally she takes him by the arm and marches up the stairs and opens the door to his room. Right on the wall there is a big stick figure. The little boy is at the age where he has noticed the difference between moms and dads so he has put on some extras. When she sees this she is mortified and begins to spank him and tells him that she will have his father deal with him. At this point, the little boy is not being rational. He is not thinking that this is an inopportune time to show my painting to my mom. What he thinks is: "Gosh! This is the best I can do and it hurts." He grows up not ever wanting to try to paint again. It is too painful. He has accumulated many rocks on the negative side of his attitudinal balance scale. An attitude has been formed. Who were the experts? Five-year-old sister, nine-year-old brother and a distraught mother. It had nothing to do with talent.

Sometimes attitudes are formed by words, pictures, feelings; but other times by our own self-talk. I am asked to stand in front of a group of my peers to explain a procedure with which I am very familiar. I get nervous and forget what I am expected to say. I begin to talk to myself. "Nice going, stupid, you always blow it when you stand in front of a group." My own self-talk triggers pictures which brings about feelings.

1. Why do we form bad attitudes (habits)? At first we didn't know that it was bad. (Youngsters begin smoking because peers do it, therefore, it must be good.)

2. We lock on to the best of several undesirable alternatives.

I have been assigned to make a speech in school. But the night before the cows break out of the pasture and I am up until midnight getting them back into the pasture. The next day I am called upon and I tell the teacher that I am not prepared. You'd think that World War III had broken out. So the next time I have to make a speech I will stay up to midnight preparing the speech. The next day when I stand in front of the class my knees begin to shake, my hands shake, my voice cracks, I sweat, and my peers laugh me off the floor. The next time I am required to make a speech I will pretend to be sick and skip school. Thereafter, whenever I am required to do something challenging I will get sick and skip.

One might ask how can we evaluate present attitudes

(habits)? We need to:

1. Recognize that they were originally formed to achieve some sort of satisfaction.

2. Determine exactly what that satisfaction is.

3. Substitute a more effective and desirable attitude.

Attitudes cannot be erased; however, they can be displaced. Let me illustrate. Let's assume that you have a glass filled to the brim with water and you have a pile of rocks. When we drop a rock into the water the water is displaced. As we continue to drop rocks into the glass of water the water continues to be displaced. We will never get rid of all the water, but we will end up with more rocks than water. We can displace old negative attitudes with positive success attitudes. Let's once again look at the attitudinal balance scale.

If we have a hundred pounds of rocks on the negative side of our attitudinal balance scale and we begin to pile rocks on the positive side, we then must add more than a hundred pounds to the positive side before it begins to move. But when we get it to leaning toward the positive side we haven't gotten rid of those on the negative side. That's why you can't stop putting weights on the positive side. Even though it's leaning in that direction we achieve balance or rebalance through repetition and accumulation of many experiences and feelings.

One might ask why don't we change our negative attitudes?

1. Fear (of the unknown).

2. Indecision (why change even if it's better).

Bill Gothard said: "The good things in life are often the mortal enemies of the best things in life."

For example: *Good health.* I take it for granted and through my eating habits, smoking, and lack of exercise, I abuse it. I have a heart attack and I develop sane living habits. I eat the proper foods. I quit smoking. I begin to exercise.

Remember an attitude is the direction in which we lean either toward or away from something. It's a habit of thought. Self-image is the accumulation of all the attitudes and opinions I have perceived about myself since birth. Subconscious pictures about myself that control my performance. We have separate images in each individual area of my life.

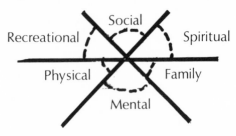

The figure that appears above is called a star graph. As you can see if I were to extend the lines into infinity not only would they get longer but also farther apart. That represents my potential in any of these areas. No one can tell me my potential in any of these areas. I can't even tell myself. I only know that I can be much more than I am. I can't measure my potential but I can measure my effectiveness. The dotted lines represent effectiveness. It is our thesis that the reason for such a difference in potential and effectiveness is because of my *self-image*. My image can be high or low in any of the areas. Let's examine how this works.

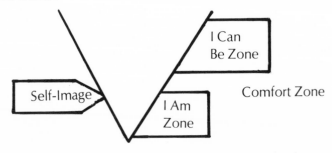

We have a regulating mechanism inside of us that controls performance just like a thermostat controls temperature. If I set the thermostat on 70° the heating mechanism goes on and the fan begins to blow warm air into the room. The temperature continues to rise until it gets to approximately 72° at which time it shuts off and the temperature begins to cool down until it gets to 68°. Then it ignites again and begins to blow warm air until it gets to 72°. Now suppose I want the temperature to be 80°? I leave the thermostat set at 70° and I light a fire in the fireplace. The temperature begins to rise 68-69-70-71-72-73-74 — at this time the air conditioner goes on and begins to blow cold air to get it back down to 70°. So if I want the temperature to be 80° I must set the thermostat on 80°; then the temperature will follow. The same is true with performance. To get performance to change we want first to change the image and performance will follow. Frequently because of performance we will move employees up the administrative ladder to supervisor, department head, vice president or administrator, or whatever. But they fall flat on their face. Why? Because their image is still down with their previous position and they creatively try to get back *where they belong.* It's the bicep-tricep concept that we discussed in chapter two. The "truth" about me is stored in my subconscious and my creative subconscious makes me act like that "truth." We have mentioned the term "comfort zone." Let's define it. *It is that zone which corresponds to my current self-image in any particular area of my life. I effectively and efficiently perform tasks and skills in this area. Performing outside of this zone usually lowers performance and causes anxiety and stress.*

I am promoted to a management position. I am now required to attend social gatherings with the board and doctors. My image is one of discomfort in the presence of these kinds of people. I am asked to stand in front of the group and explain future plans to the group. I am out of my comfort zone and when I attempt to speak my mouth becomes dry, my vocal cords tighten and my voice cracks. I begin to perspire and shake. I can hardly talk. I am not acting like my subconscious picture of me so my creative subconscious says: "Get back where you belong." My self-talk takes over and I begin to emotionally beat myself.

It's like walking an 18-inch wide plank. As long as it's on the floor I have no problem walking the plank. But, put that plank 100 feet above the ground and try to walk the plank. All of a sudden the plank becomes much more narrow. Anxiety and stress set in and performance goes down. We begin to imagine ourself as falling and soon we feel pulled toward the fall. This simply illustrates one of our concepts. It is commonly referred to as the "strangest secret in the world." We move toward and become like those things which we think about all the time; therefore, if we continue to think about that which we don't want, that's what we get. As I walk the plank while it is on the ground, it is easy to walk because the only thing that I am thinking about is walking the length of the plank. However, when it is 100 feet above the ground I am thinking about falling. The same is true about any and all of my thoughts. I am scheduled to make a presentation before a group. If I continue to think about failure it is almost certain that I will. My creative subconscious will make me act like that picture that I hold of myself. I must hold the picture of that which I want — not that which I don't want. For example: If I tell you, "Don't think about a banana. That's right, don't think about a banana." What picture is in your mind? That's right — a banana. If I tell my kid: "Don't spill the milk," what do they see? They see spilt milk. Or I tell an employee, "Don't be late," or "Don't forget." What do they see? *Be late* and *forget*. So we want to get in the habit of telling ourselves and others what we want — not what we don't want. If we want our children to arrive at the table with the glass full, then that's what we want to affirm. If I want them to remember, then that's what I affirm. If I want to make a good presentation, then I want to get in the habit of dwelling upon my making a good presentation, not on the fact that I may blow it. If I am to administer to a discipline problem, I see myself functioning as a calm, cool individual who handles all situations very calmly and coolly. Rather than one who loses his cool and blows it. Let's refer back to our illustration of the thermostat. As we set the thermostat to 70° the temperature will follow either up or down depending upon the setting of the thermostat. Homosapiens are controlled by tension and stress similar to a thermostat except we are not controlled electrically. My self-image is a subconscious picture (or setting) of *where I should be*. We refer to this as our currently dominant image of reality about us. We, just like the thermostat, have an *area of flexibility*. When we set the thermostat on 70° it fluctuates between 68° and 72°. This is its area of flexibility — 4°. Also, like the thermostat whenever we find ourselves either below or above this zone, which corresponds with our self-image, tension and anxiety occur, sending us a message to raise or lower our performance.

Physical evidence of leaving our comfort zone:

1. Respiration increases and breathing becomes more of a conscious effort.
2. Knees get shaky.
3. Heart begins to palpitate.
4. Muscles in neck and shoulders become tense.
5. Our digestive juices oversecrete.
6. Palms become moist.
7. Mouth gets dry.
8. Vocal cords tighten and voice changes.
9. We begin to perspire.

The result is decreased effectiveness and poor performance.

The following is an example of how it works in making a presentation before board.

My Self-Image: Based upon past performance I "see myself" as a poor public speaker (my reality).

My Comfort Zone: Speaking in front of important groups

puts me out of my comfort zone.

My Performance Reality: When I attempt to speak in front of the board I am in conflict with my subconscious picture (reality) of me. Therefore: My creative subconscious makes me "get back where I belong."

The Result: The free flow of information is cut off from my subconscious.

— My voice cracks.

— I lose poise and confidence.

— I lose my place in the presentation.

Self-Talk: Nice going, stupid, every time you make a presentation in front of an important group *you blow it*. That's like you.

The same thing occurs when we are at a party with a social group that is different from the one with which I normally associate. This environment conflicts with my subconscious picture (reality) of me, and my creative subconscious sends me a message to get back where I belong. I might even become ill and have to leave the party. If my picture of me, as a golfer, is *I am a 100 golfer* why is it if I shoot a 40 on the front nine I creatively shoot a 60 on the back nine to "get back where I belong."

The question then is, "How can we affect a desired change in ourselves and others?"

We all have a desire to be a more effective administrator, a better public speaker, a better spouse, a better parent. There are two ways to go beyond my current self-image and comfort zone.

1. With the use of willpower I try to change performance. This is known as the traditional method of change. This method usually is very tense and stressful and causes us to become modern day cannibals; we begin to digest ourselves. It's known as a duodenal ulcer.

An example of how this works follows:

I am in Colorado Springs, CO, and I have an appointment in Denver, which is 65 miles north. It's an important appointment and I am pressed for time. I decide to get in my small plane and fly to Denver. I get up to 10,000 feet and I set the automatic pilot to fly north. I let go the wheel and begin to relax. As I begin to relax I look ahead of me and I see a large thunder cloud. If you know anything about flying then you know that the smart thing to do is to turn around and go back home. But, it is an important appointment so I decide to fly around the thunder cloud. The mountains are to the west so I decide to fly around the thunder cloud to the east. I grab the wheel of the plane and turn it toward the east. I let go of the wheel and begin to relax. The plane turns to the north back into the thunder cloud. I grab the wheel again and turn it so that the plane is once again headed east. I let go of the wheel and the plane once again turns toward the north.

Obviously what is happening is that I forgot to reprogram the automatic pilot. As long as I am holding on to the wheel of the plane I can make it go in any direction I want it to. But, when I let go of the wheel the airplane turns back toward the direction it is programmed to go.

It's like making a New Year's resolution. I resolve "not to eat sweets," so I grab hold to the steering wheel of my life (will power) and begin to grit my teeth and bust my gut and affirm, "I'm not going to eat sweets, I'm not going to eat sweets." The weekend comes and I've really done a good job so I relax (let go of the steering wheel) and I overdose on sweets. My self-image (the automatic pilot) controls my performance and so I go back to where I am programmed to go. Any time we put will-power (grab hold to the wheel) up against subconscious reality (the automatic pilot) subconscious reality always wins.

This is why if I want to become a winner or if I want to help someone else to become a winner I want to change the picture in my subconscious.

2. Change the self-image first. This is a more relaxed, less tense, more dignified method of change. We change the subconscious picture (reality) first and our performance will follow

naturally and free-flowingly. Our performance will rise to our new expectations (new self-image). Just like the example of the thermostat, we change the setting on the thermostat and the temperature follows. We change our self-image and the performance follows. We now have our creative subconscious working for us rather than against us. Our filter system is open for new information that will help us change and we have new found drive and energy.

Let's summarize:

The largest and swiftest changes take place when we change our self-image *first*.

When we change the way we see ourselves on the subconscious level we automatically change our expectations. The creative subconscious senses the disparity between our new expectations and our current performance level. It will then give us drive and energy to raise our performance and it creatively overcomes obstacles along the way. Our filter system is wide open for new information because we now know exactly what our new image demands.

When we raise our self-image, we automatically increase our comfort zone so that we are more relaxed and confident as we seek to raise our performance. Consequently we become more effective.

The challenge as I see it is to intentionally change where we *want* to be. See the *pay value* in something so clearly that we have great desire and determination to go after it. Make a deliberate decision to find out exactly what will make us happy, so that our creative energies will work for us rather than against us.

That is exactly what motivation is all about.

Who is going to be *responsible* for determining what you truly want out of life?

Who is going to motivate your staff, your employees?

Those are questions you should be asking, questions this book can help you answer.

Motivation: Leadership or Pushership?

If we have a good understanding of attitude and self-image, motivation should never be a problem.

As I was reflecting upon this chapter, I couldn't help but ask myself, "How can I communicate this topic to people so that they will know what I mean?" The longer I pondered this challenge the more convinced I became that I must relate my information to thoughts that everyone could understand. I thought to myself, "If I were a taxi driver, how would I motivate people to ride in my taxi rather than someone else's taxi?" I also thought, "If I were a door-knob salesman, how would I motivate people to want to turn my door-knobs rather than someone else's?"

These thoughts might seem strange to you, but actually that's what motivation is all about. If we are to be considered as leaders, and this is what we are, we need to understand that it's not what we know or believe to be true, but rather what we are able to convince others is true. If we are to be leaders we need to have someone following us.

If my object is to motivate you and I do so, and I get you very excited and enthusiastic and then I leave you, I have done you a great disservice. However, if I provide you with the tool to motivate yourself then I have done you a great service. The type of motivation that we will share with you is the type that motivates you to want to motivate yourself.

Back to the taxi and door-knobs. If I tell you that if you ride in my taxi and if you turn my door-knobs you'll really get "turned on" it is very likely that I'd talk forever and not be able to convince you that what I was selling was true. But suppose I told you that some of your oldest and dearest friends had planned a surprise party for you and they had been planning it for over a year. They had all of your favorite drinks, your favorite foods, your favorite desserts, your favorite games and furthermore they had all chipped in and bought you a present, one that you have always wanted but could not afford. You'd ride in 10 taxi cabs and turn all kinds of door-knobs to get to the party. So what am I trying to communicate to you? You don't ride in taxi cabs to get "turned on," and you don't turn door-knobs to get "turned on." You ride in taxi cabs to get from one location to another location. You turn door-knobs to get on the other side of the door. What, you ask, does this have to do with motivation? If we want to motivate people to want to motivate themselves we need to be able to paint the big picture, the end result. What is the "pay value?" What's in it for me?

Follow me through this example. A high school football coach meets with his team and this is what he tells them: "Well guys I'm sorry to have to tell you this but our budget didn't pass the school board and we have no money. We have to cancel our schedule. There will be no games, no band, no cheerleaders, and no crowd. But we would like all of you to remain on the team. We will meet behind the gym every afternoon and practice hitting each other. You'll really love it!"

I don't think we would have a very large "turn out."

Have you noticed what a lousy job your son does when cutting your lawn? The very minimum of effort, no trim, no raking. Just cutting and then he misses much of it. But notice the great job he does when he cuts his girl friend's lawn. He trims it, rakes it, puts grass in plastic bags and takes it out for the trash man to pick up. Different picture entirely.

Now, back to the football coach. Suppose he told his team: "Well, guys, your season has been cut. But wait, all is not lost.

We are scheduling a series of intrasquad games. And we'll have cheerleaders and the band, and we'll make admittance free of charge. We should get some of the largest crowds ever to watch you. Practice starts tomorrow, and I expect you all there."

The football coach has learned the secret of motivation. He has learned to paint the picture of the cheerleaders, the band, mothers and dads and brothers and sisters and friends. Everyone will be there yelling and screaming for you.

The pay value for your son cutting his girl friend's lawn well? So her mom and dad won't be quite so angry if they come in late. Or he will become such a fine young man in their eye maybe they will agree to let the couple stay out later.

Neither one of the above is focusing on the task at hand. The hard sweaty practices or the lawn cutting. They are focused on the end result, the pay value.

How, you say, does this apply to the custodial staff, the secretarial staff, the laundry room? I think that the challenge is no different. We need to be able to paint the big picture for them and this will vary from area to area, from one hospital to another. We want to keep the picture of the benefits involved in working for this particular organization. Hospitals have a built-in reward system and seldom take advantage of it. There is a built in *purpose:* "When you clean the floors, walls, laundry or whatever, you are eliminating infection which transfers directly to the patient." You have a sense of being needed by someone who is in need, someone who is hurting. You then become an integral part of the healing process.

Another key to motivation and to growth is what Abraham Maslow refers to as the four levels of learning I referred to in Chapter One. Let's review these. The first level of learning is the *unconscious incompetent,* which simply means we are stupid and don't know it. The second level is the *conscious incompetent,* which means we are stupid and we do know it. The third level is the *conscious competent,* which means we know how to do it and we know we know. The fourth level is the *unconscious competent,* which means we do it so we don't have to think about it while doing it.

Take the act of hitting a golf ball. When we are youngsters we are unconscious incompetents. When it comes to hitting a golf ball we don't know how to hold the golf club, tee the ball, swing the club, follow through. In other words we know nothing about hitting a golf ball and we don't even know that we don't know. We now go out to the golf course and we tee the ball and take out the club (we don't even know which club), we swing at the ball and miss it entirely. We have now become a *conscious incompetent.* We then decide to take lessons and in a short period of time we become a *conscious competent.* We can hit the ball with a relative degree of accuracy, but we are still on the conscious level. We need to think about every move. As we continue to practice and play we soon become an *unconscious competent.* We don't think about the swing. As a matter of fact if we begin to think about our actions during the swing we "blow it."

How does this principle apply to motivation? We take people and expose them to information which causes them to become unconscious incompetents. We then begin to provide them with data to assist them in moving through the four levels of learning. Once they have successfully moved through the four levels of learning we once again expose them to new information which causes them to become unconscious incompetents. We begin the process again; then we are providing them with the opportunity for growth and the tools that assist them in this growth.

Generally speaking we are at our physical peak between the ages of 21 and 35. At about age 35 we usually are where we want to be or we know we are going to get there or we know we are not going to make it. We usually find ourselves in one of these three situations around age 35. I am mentioning this also because it is helpful to understand this so that I have another tool to motivate myself and others. We all have a purpose line or goal line. We strive to achieve this purpose. We also have a life line. The purpose line or goal line is horizontal; whereas the life line is somewhat diagonal. If the life line begins to tail off at about age 35 and if our life line and purpose line meet at this time the life line will pull the purpose line down with it. In terms of death, it is instant, not necessarily physical death but we quit growing. The only evidence of life is growth. So one of the keys to growth, life, motivation is to continue to elevate the purpose line every three or four years. This causes us to continue to reach, stretch, and grow. The creative thrust is the key to life.

Never sanction incompetence for any reason, at any time or at any place. The way to sanction incompetence is to ignore it. If we don't sanction incompetence then we need to teach people how not to be incompetent. The way to teach people how not to be incompetent is first have them do the task (work). Secondly, teach the skills necessary to perform the task with competence; and thirdly, by being the model that you wish them to emulate.

Most of us go through life on a "have to" basis. I have to do this; I must do this and such; I ought to, I should do this, I have to fill in this report; I should go to work; I ought to take my spouse to dinner; I must go to church. There are only two "have to's" in your life. They are death and choice. I don't "have to" work. I could go on welfare. I don't "have to" pay taxes. I could leave the country or go to prison. Since these are not "have to's" they are "choose to's," and since they are "choose to's" they are "want to's." If I choose to do something I am saying I want to do it. It might not be high on my priority list but I choose to do it rather than accept the consequences. I don't like to pay taxes; but I pay taxes rather than accept the consequences, prison. Why don't I quit intimidating and coercing myself and others by saying I have to do this or you have to do that? Because, when someone tells me I have to do something I "push back." When I tell me I have to do something I "push back." Our greatest power is our power to choose. We have no greater power but yet we spend most of our life denying that we have it when we tell ourself: "I have to." It is a super "put down." We are taking away our own accountability for change. We are saying I am not accountable. I must do what they tell me.

Let's take a look at the two styles of motivation. There is *restrictive* motivation, which is based on coercion or inhibition. I don't want to but I have to. I want to but I can't. Restrictive motivation is a negative style of motivation and there is always an "or else" factor. You cut the lawn "or else." You get that report in on time "or else." Restrictive motivation is motivation through fear. All kinds of fear, fear of rejection, fear of ridicule, fear of embarrassment, fear of sarcasm, fear of punishment. This kind of motivation is not leadership. It's *pushership*. We are pushing people into change. We are taking away their accountability to change.

Remember the old expression: "If at first you don't succeed try, try again." This expression has been changed by the people who are motivated restrictively. They say: "If at first you don't succeed, fix the blame fast." People who are motivated on "have to" are always fixing the blame. I didn't do it well. It's because you didn't make me. The reason I'm not motivated is because they didn't motivate me. *Restrictively motivated people:*

● Fix the blame.
● Find excuses.
● Must be constantly pushed.
● Give up accountability for their decisions.
● Lack drive and energy.
● Push back.

Consequently, they develop a losing attitude. They focus on the loss rather than the win. "What if I give a party and nobody comes?"

The constructive style of motivation is based on *"I want to."* Within the construction style there are two types of motivation: incentive and attitudinal achievement. The incentive motivation is based on a reward system. It is extrinsic motivation, from the outside. Some examples are retirement insurance, health insurance, trip to Hawaii. I will do the task for the reward. I want the reward but not the task. When we are motivated on an incentive basis it soon becomes an expectation. Once it becomes an expectation it no longer is an incentive. Therefore, we need to continue to raise the incentive to get the same performance repeated. We need to remember that we are not all motivated by the same incentive. Some people might want a trip to some exotic island; others might want to drive a pink Cadillac; still others might want to travel to Europe. Therefore, if you want to motivate people with an incentive it's necessary to have many different incentives. The other type of motivation within the constructive style is known as attitudinal motivation. Attitudinal motivation is the kind of motivation that people with hobbies have; they just love to do it. They enjoy the task.

Several years ago my family went on a week long camping trip. We went camping on Orcas Island. Orcas Island is in northern San Juan — in Puget Sound off the coast of Washington. This island abounds in seafood of all kinds. That morning our family had gone out crabbing and, also, clamming. As a result we caught many crabs and dug many clams. We were all very excited. My wife and I were busy getting things ready for dinner. We wanted to boil the crabs so we needed some wood for a fire. My wife and I and several of the kids were cleaning the clams so that we could put them in the ice box. I had told my kids that we were going to go fishing. Some of our kids really like to go fishing. Others could care less. So here we are hustling trying to get things ready for dinner so that we could go fishing. Several of our kids were helping us to get ready by cleaning the clams. These are the kids that look for ways to help so that we can get done what needs to be done.

We needed someone to cut wood so that we could start the water boiling to boil the crabs. One of our sons was standing around doing nothing. I told him to cut the wood so that we could boil the crabs and go fishing. This particular son didn't particularly care for fishing. I noticed that he wasn't cutting the wood, so I asked what was wrong. He said that he couldn't find the ax. I pointed out to him that he was standing on the ax. He picked up the ax and was swinging it about every 30 seconds. At this rate we would never have enough wood. I then told one of our sons, who was three years younger, but loved to fish, to go and cut the wood so that we could go fishing. You can't believe how fast this young kid cut wood. We had enough wood cut to boil those crabs in 10 minutes. Those kids that were helping just because they wanted to were motivated attitudinally. The kid that cut the wood did so because he was motivated through incentive. We finally motivated the other boy restrictively by restricting his water skiing the next day.

Constructively motivated people see the pay value, they want to, whereas restrictively motivated people always have to be pushed, intimidated, coerced into doing things. Constructively motivated people:

- Are self-starters.
- Accept accountability.
- Look for solutions not excuses.
- Have tremendous drive and energy.

They develop a winning attitude. (What if I throw a party and everyone comes?)

In *restrictive motivation,* my creative subconscious works against me. I creatively move away from that which I don't want or fear.

In *constructive motivation,* my creative subconscious works for me. I creatively move with drive and energy towards that which I ardently desire.

Steps to growth and learning (constructive model):

1. Clearly see, taste and feel the desired change already occurring, and the reasons why I want to (pay value).

2. Gather correct information and skills.

3. Allow myself and others to make mistakes, and then learn from them. (Know that setbacks are only temporary feedback to signal that I am off course.) (Monitor and adjust.)

4. Repeat, repeat, repeat.

Practice of perfection makes perfect. (Conscious practice eventually becomes subconscious skills.) The key to motivation is:

- Pay value.
- Personal profitability.
- Seeing and wanting a desired end result for ourselves.

The biggest single variable is *pay value*. Once I decide what's important in my life, and see a clear, vivid picture in my mind, my creative mechanism will take over, the result is *burning desire; excitement; adventure; enthusiasm for a course of action.*

The same principles apply in motivating our staff members and co-workers.

How many times have we:

- Introduced a new skill to our staff by telling them it's going to be difficult, or it's very expensive, or perhaps: "It's the best under these circumstances?"
- Told staff that we had better work harder so that we won't get fired?
- Began a new year by telling our staff: "It's not going to be easy?"

If we want to motivate our staff with dignity, we want to first help them to see the pay value. (What's in it for them.)
When introducing a new task, a new skill, etc.

1. We want first to make certain that the people we are motivating are *relaxed* (If they are nervous, threatened or apprehensive, very little learning takes place; without learning no

motivation. We want to move them from the unconscious incompetent level.)

2. *Fascination:* Break through the boredom barrier. Show them something new, different, better. Build up suspense; make them a promise that will later be fulfilled. Very little learning takes place without attention. That's why fascination is so very important.

3. Help them *visualize* both the end result and pay value.

- What is this new thing?
- Why do we want to do it?
- How do we want to do it?
- Why is it fun, interesting, valuable, exciting?
- Is there anything to fear or dislike in this new thing?
- What will it be like when we are finished?
- How will we be happier, better, safer, smarter, healthier?
- Who else has done this thing?
- Did they like it?
- What did they get out of it?
- Is everyone going to do this new thing?
- Am I going to be involved?
- When do we start?
- How will we know if we are progressing?
- When will we finish?

In the long run constructive motivation based on pay value is far less demanding and produces far more exciting results.

Disciplined Imagination: Believing Is Seeing

While reading newspapers and watching television we see that human potential is almost unlimited. Much of our research backs this up. But research also points out that even the greatest of geniuses use only a very small amount of their ability. It is generally agreed that most of our limitations are self-imposed. We are totally a product of our conditioning, and some of our conditioning is very good. On the other hand much of our conditioning, as we have suggested, has been founded on "garbage in."

To become more productive, more effective administrators we need tools to pick us out of our "rut."

When we discussed our thought process we mentioned that we perceived our environment through our senses and everything we perceived, we perceived to be true. Our subconscious *stored* this "truth" and our creative subconscious maintained this "truth." What makes me act like me is my subconscious picture of me.

We then examined attitudes. Our attitudes are formed through conditioning, self-talk (words → picture → feelings) and also opinions of society. Since we developed our present attitudes through conditioning (words → picture → feelings) we can develop new attitudes (habits of thought) through our controlled self-talk. It is true that we cannot erase old attitudes but we can displace them through deliberate input.

Let us examine what we mean by displacement by reviewing our water glass analogy. Imagine a glass of water that is filled to the brim. If we have a pile of rocks and we take one of the rocks and drop it into the glass filled with water the water will be displaced by the rock. If we continued to do that we would find that each time we would drop a rock we would continue to displace the water. We would never displace *all* of the water in the glass however. We would end up with more rocks than water. That's what we mean by displacing old attitudes. We will never get rid of the old attitudes but we can create a new dominant "reality."

My self-image is simply an accumulation of all of my attitudes. I have an image of who I am and how I expect myself to act in all areas of my life. This image is stored in my subconscious as truth and my creative subconscious makes me act like that image, regardless of my potential. We have discovered that my self-image determines my *comfort zone*. This is the area in which I operate effectively and efficiently. Anytime I perform either above or below my comfort zone I experience tension and distress, which in turn causes me either to increase my performance, to get up where I belong, or get back down where I belong. My current self-image controls my performance.

Essentially there are two ways to change. I can choose to change my self-image and have my performance follow. This is the dignified method of change. I accomplish this without creating anxiety or distress. The other method of change is to change my performance and hope for my self-image to follow. This method is most distressful and causes anxiety and stress. We are working against our creative subconscious. Take the example I used earlier of me in my plane going to Denver and setting the automatic pilot. As long as I controlled the steering mechanism I could make the plane go in any direction I chose; but when I let go the plane would go in the direction that it was programmed to go.

Weight control is another example. People will loose weight for a short time by consciously sticking to a certain diet. As soon as they have lost a little weight, they let go of the steering wheel and the automatic pilot subconsciously moves them back to their old self-image. (I am the kind of person who is usually overweight.)

In other words, changing the self-image is like changing the setting on the automatic pilot. Once I have changed the setting my plane will automatically head in that direction. Many of our images about ourself have been formed by garbage in, by the negative or devaluative opinions that other people have given about my performance. These opinions are not always the truth but only someone else's opinion. To the degree that my image is founded on misinformation, then my corresponding behavior or actions will also be unwise or inaccurate. Remember the art story and how the little child formed a negative attitude about art? It had nothing to do with ability but through words, pictures, and feelings of others a negative attitude was formed. I remember when I was thirteen one of my friends got angry with me and called me a "big nose." I don't know whether or not I have a big nose but each time I look in a mirror I see a big nose.

How many times have you had the same thing happen to you? How much of our present image is an accurate reflection of what we *can* be?

How much garbage in have you accepted from other people? What have you *imagined* to be *true* about yourself? Imagination is so very powerful. To the degree that we vividly imagine and feel an experience, it is stored in our subconscious as *truth* and *reality* and is later used as *true* information. Imagination times vividness = reality in our subconscious.

When I was in college I was a member of the football team. When you lettered in a sport you could be invited to join the "L" club. I was asked to join. To become a member of the "L" club you were required to go through an initiation. Prior to going through the initiation the candidates were shown some of the things that they would be required to do. They gave you an opportunity to refuse, because once you started through the initiation they would not allow you to quit.

One of the things that they showed us was a can of worms. We would be required to select a worm and eat it. I looked around and waited to see who would drop out but no one did, so I didn't either. They also showed us a huge tarantula spider in a jar. They told us that we would be required to take our shirts off and lie on our backs and allow the spider to crawl across our chest. They reminded us that the spider was very nervous and if we moved at all the spider might bite us. Once again I waited for someone to drop out but no one did. So I didn't either. We were then all blindfolded and we started the initiation. When we came to the worms we were required to reach into the can and select a worm and chew it and eat it. I don't think that I have ever done anything more difficult than that. I even vomited.

When it was time to allow the spider to crawl across our bare chest I was so frightened I almost passed out. I took off my shirt and got on the floor on my back whereupon they put the spider on my chest. I held my breath, because I didn't want to move. The spider moved across my bare chest ever so slowly. Finally, I had to take a breath and the spider bit me on my chest. I immediately ripped off the blindfold and jumped up and there was a huge welt on my chest. I thought I was going to die. The truth about this entire scene is I actually had eaten a piece of spaghetti with dirt on it. Why did I vomit? Because *my subconscious does not know the difference between a real experience and a vividly imagined experience accompanied with feelings.*

The spider was not a spider at all. It was an apple with tooth picks stuck in it and they rolled it across my chest. The bite was candle wax dripped on my chest. Once again my subconscious did not know the difference so I developed a welt on my chest.

In the examples above I accepted misinformation (garbage

in) as truth. Accepting and allowing our imagination to run wild only perpetuates low self-image. So let's begin to use our imagination in a positive rather than negative way.

In the summer of 1956 I had the greatest spectator experience of my life. Along with my oldest son Morris, who was seven years old, I attended the Olympic Time Trials. They were held at the Los Angeles Coliseum. It was a week long event and 70 to 80 thousand people were in attendance. In 1956 the United States had no peer in track and field, so seeing the time trials was almost as spectacular as seeing the Olympics. What a thrill to be able to witness this great spectacle with my son. We were both speechless.

Wednesday was a night meet and it was late in the evening. Most of the competitors were through competing and most of the spectators had left the coliseum. On the floor of the coliseum was a beautiful young man whose name is Charles Dumas. Charles was a high jumper. The bar was set at seven feet — *the impossible barrier.* This is what the "experts" said. No man would ever high jump seven feet. Charles did jump seven feet that night. The next day when they interviewed Charles they asked him: "Had you ever jumped seven feet in practice?" He said he never had. They then asked him: "How did you prepare yourself for this accomplishment?" Charles told them that he had measured seven feet up the wall in his bedroom and put some masking tape there to represent the high jump bar at seven feet. Charles told them that each time he looked at that masking tape he could just *feel* himself going over the bar. He said that he must have gone over the bar five thousand times in his mind. Charles was using disciplined imagination. He began to see himself as a seven foot high jumper. Once this new "truth" was established and stored in his subconscious, his creative subconscious worked to maintain this "reality."

Several years ago I was watching two college football teams playing on television. On this particular play a back carried the ball and gained nine yards. When he was tackled he then fumbled. The camera zoomed in on him and showed him pounding the turf with his fist with great emotion. He then got up and kicked the turf with great emotion. The camera followed him to the bench where he threw his helmet down to the ground with great emotion. He then threw his hands up in the air with great emotion. Let's examine what went on; he carried the ball and gained nine yards. He was tackled and fumbled. Now that's one fumble. He pounded the turf with great emotion. That's two fumbles. He kicked the turf. That's three fumbles. He went to the bench and threw his helmet to the ground. That's four fumbles. He then threw his hands into the air. That's five fumbles. Our subconscious cannot tell the difference between a real experience and one that is vividly imagined accompanied with emotion. To the degree that we vividly imagine and feel and experience it is stored in our subconscious as "truth" and "reality" and later used as "true" information. Each time he vividly imagined himself as fumbling, it was the same as if he actually was doing it. He then *saw* himself as a fumbler. Consequently he became a fumbler.

"When I stand in front of a group to talk I get so nervous I can't remember what it is I wanted to say." Sure enough each time I say that to myself and I imagine myself as doing what I said, I am living the failure and I soon become like me to "blow it" when I stand in front of a group.

I want to be very careful of what I am affirming and imagining to myself because my subconscious does not evaluate it. I accept it as true information. Knowing this I can turn it around and begin to use my imagination so that it works for me and not against me. I now begin to visualize myself as standing in front of a group and really turning them on. As I continuously imagine myself doing this I begin to see myself as a person who is very relaxed and dynamic in front of a group. Eventually this becomes the "truth" about me that is stored in my subconscious. My creative subconscious now makes me act like this new me.

One can use this technique (tool) when communicating with his or her spouse or employees. The same is true when disciplinary action is necessary with an employee or with one's child. Whatever the task, I can vividly imagine myself performing it perfectly over and over again. This soon becomes the "truth" about me stored in my subconscious. I now feel very comfortable and I perform very effectively and efficiently.

If I choose to grow and become, I can use positive imagination to create a new subconscious picture for myself. I can begin changing the self-image regulator (automatic pilot) by changing what I imagine or expect of myself on the subconscious level. Only vivid images that I experience personally will change my subconscious picture.

If I clearly and vividly imagine myself in the *first person*, being, doing, having the things and qualities I truly want, then I am using positive imagination to begin my change. The more *clearly* and *vividly* I imagine my new environment with repetition and feeling, the stronger and more real the pictures on the subconscious level. Once the subconscious accepts this new image my creative subconscious goes to work to maintain it. Practicing in the imagination is the proper use and now accepted use of the soundest psychological and physiological principles.

Steps to using positive imagination
A. Get a clear picture of end result. What do I want?
B. Imagine the end result in specific vivid detail.
C. See myself in the first person experiencing the desired end.
   (If I set a goal to go to Hawaii with my family I want to vividly imagine myself as standing on the beach with my family. I feel the warm sand on my feet, the warm sun on my body. I smell the salt air, I see the blue sky and blue ocean. I hear the waves breaking in the surf line, I taste the salt on my lips.)
D. Repeat over and over.
E. Lock out negative and conflicting pictures.

Remember practice does not make perfect. Practice of perfection makes perfect, and the only way we can be assured of perfection is in our imagination.

I can practice hitting a golf ball perfectly every time in my imagination. I can practice administering to any and every situation perfectly in my imagination.

We program and condition ourselves every day through active use of our imagination.

1. We can do it randomly or with purpose.

2. We can do it positively or negatively.

3. We can deliberately imagine new expectations for ourselves, or allow others to do it for us.

Do I imagine myself winning or losing?

Do I imagine myself being happy or sad?

Do I imagine good days or bad days?

Do I imagine opportunities in every difficulty or do I imagine difficulties in every opportunity?

Am I doubting my beliefs and believing my doubts, or am I believing my beliefs and doubting my doubts.

Winners see what they want, losers see what they don't want.

We are talking about raising our self-image in order to improve our performance in a desired area of life.

Through positive use of my imagination I can project my own future. I can "see myself" already enjoying the desired change. If the picture is vivid and detailed and if I trigger it often enough, it will be impressed into my subconscious as my new image.

This causes a positive conflict between "what is" and "what should be" (cognitive dissonance).

My creative subconscious will then work to bring that new image to completion for me.

Self-A-Steam: The Achievement Switch

I think that the greatest need we have in our modern "civilized" society is self-esteem. The reason that I write "civilized" society is because in "uncivilized" society we find high self-esteem. This being the case it seems logical to conclude that it must be something in our society that is contributing to our low self-esteem.

Much of what follows is based on data that I have observed. As a result I have come to some conclusions.

I think that children who grow up believing that they evolved from an ape don't get too excited about that possibility. Nor do I. However, when I believe that I was created in the image and likeness of God I do get excited. I think that this might have a bearing on one's self-esteem. Have you noticed what television commercials are doing to us? Most commercials are a total put down. Many advertising campaigns are based on the premise that we believe we are our bodies. Therefore, they point out what might be considered imperfections in our bodies and cause us to believe that this is bad. If we believe that we are our bodies and our bodies are bad then we can't feel good about ourselves.

For example: We have body odor, foot odor, bad breath, split ends, the greasies, ring around the collar. If we buy certain products we will be cured. So we buy these products and we still have "ring around the collar." I must really be no good. Even the products don't help me.

Frequently children are brought up to believe that love is

conditional or that *things* are more important than *people*. We have a young child and we love that child. We embrace that child, we nurture that child. Then that child leaves our arms and goes outside and picks up a rock and throws it through a window. All too frequently that child is spanked and told, "You are a bad little boy or girl." The child then begins to wonder. Five minutes ago you told me you loved me. Now you spank me and tell mè I am bad. You can't love anything that's bad. If that's what love is all about I don't want any. The child drops his/her plate on the way to the table and he/she gets punished. Things are more important than people. All of these things have a bearing on self-esteem. Children also learn they are their actions. I am my actions. I am good when my actions are good. I am bad when my actions are bad. What needs to be done is separate the person from the act. This doesn't mean that we ignore the act, but in the case of children we don't demean or devalue a person because of their act. If we have discussed with the child consequences of a type of action, then we carry out the consequences. If, on the other hand, we have not previously discussed consequences, then that is the time to do it. Something like this might be said. *Honey, you know I love you and nothing that you could ever do would cause me not to love you. But we cannot tolerate that behavior.* The same for those people that we lead. We should let them know that we are not being critical of them as a person but rather the act.

I do not believe that we were created to injure one another. I believe that we were created to love one another. Therefore, if I injure one of my fellow human beings I think that I am acting less than human. If I am acting less than human I must then ask myself: "Who am I?" I am reminded of a story that I read several years ago. It was about a world famous stone sculptor. This stone sculptor had just finished carving a life-size elephant out of granite. At the unveiling the art critics were astonished at its beauty and realism. They asked: "How do you do it, how do you make it look so real?" He responded: "It's really quite simple. I simply chip away everything that doesn't look like an elephant."

In answering the question, "Who am I?" we need to first chip away everything that does not look like us. So I ask myself questions such as: Am I my body? No, I am not my body. My body is nothing more than a vehicle to transport me through this physical existence. Without legs, arms, or other parts of my body I would not be diminished one iota as to who I am. Am I my mind? No, I am not my mind. My mind is a computer that dictates to my body. My mind functions at a particular level of awareness. Am I my awareness? No, I am not my awareness. I am that which is aware. For if I were my awareness the moment that I went to sleep I would cease to exist. Awareness is defined as how clearly I perceive and understand everything that affects my life. It is the automatic product of my entire life experiences. Even though awareness is in a continual state of flux, at the moment of any decision it is absolutely fixed. Therefore, at that moment that's where my awareness was and it was the only decision that I could have made. There need not be any shame, blame, guilt or remorse. Am I my action? No, I am not my actions. I am that which acts. My actions are nothing more than the means my current awareness selects to satisfy my needs. Now that I have chipped away all of those things that are not me I am free to discover who I am.

If I am to be successful in any area of my life — career, family, physical, mental, spiritual, recreational — it is essential that I know who I am and feel good about who I am. That's what self-esteem is. How warm, friendly and appreciative I feel about myself, in spite of my weaknesses, shortcomings and human frailties is not egotism. Our self-image is the *picture* we have of ourselves in our subconscious. Our self-esteem is how we *feel* about ourselves on the subconscious level.

Our basic need is to feel good about ourselves mentally, physically, and emotionally. All of our goals, hopes and aspirations are based on this fundamental need. Genuine peace and happiness is only possible to the degree that we feel good about ourselves, in spite of our mistakes and failures.

A person who does not love or approve of himself cannot be happy nor can he love or approve of others. The source of love for others is love of self. A selfish egotistical person actually hates himself and cannot love others. Feeling good about yourself spills over and touches everyone you come in contact with. We love others in direct proportion to how much we love ourselves.

The Bible says: "Love your neighbor as thyself." The problem is *we do*. We don't love ourselves very much and we love our neighbor just like that. Lack of self-love is the root cause of a great deal of mental illness, emotional upset and suicide.

Suppose you had a friend who would give you a karate chop in the adams apple each time you walked up to him. Then he would knee you in the groin. As you start to walk away from the punch you get hit in the kidneys. Certainly you wouldn't want to be around that person very long. Well, that is what many of us do to ourselves. We continually demean and devalue ourselves through our own self-talk. *Why am I so stupid? If only I woulda, I shoulda, I coulda. I don't think I can do it. This is going to be tough. What's the matter with me? Why do I always?* These are the type of phrases that we want to eliminate from our vocabulary.

Frequently we perpetuate our own low self-esteem with our own self-talk. For example I drive to work each morning. My home is 10 miles from my work. On the way to work I pass 5,000 other cars — each one a potential accident. But, I arrive safely. Do I get excited? Do I congratulate myself for having performed as I expected or do I ignore the fact that I performed up to my expectation? Generally it's the latter. But what if on the way to work you reach over into the glove box to get something and the car in front of you stops unexpectedly and you pile into the back end of that car? We really talk to ourselves then don't we? *How could I be so stupid? What a jack-ass! Why didn't I pay attention to where I was going?* Etc. . .

We ignore our performance when it lives up to expectation but when performance does not live up to expectation we demean ourselves thereby perpetuating our own low self-esteem.

Loving and respecting ourselves is very important. The results are dignity, worthwhile, belonging, healthy humility. Eight characteristics of *sound self-esteem,* have been listed by Dr. Stanley Coopersmith.

It seems to me that these are the characteristics that we want to build into those persons who work with us in our environment:

1. When one sees oneself as valuable, important, and worthy of the respect of others, then one sees oneself as a contributor. (What we want to do is provide people with the opportunity to contribute and let them know how valuable they are.)

2. Help them get an optimistic outlook toward the future. (Don't allow others to spew garbage in the environment. Point out the positive things.)

3. Stress they are capable of influencing others and controlling their own destiny. (Provide them with opportunities to lead — such as conducting a meeting.)

4. Stress they are capable of expressing themselves and know others respect their point of view. (Ask for their opinion.)

5. Stress that they have a good awareness of their values and know that the decisions they make will be based on those values.

6. Help them enjoy new challenges and accept all set-backs as temporary. (Provide them with new challenges; don't let them remain at the unconscious competent stage.)

7. Help them find pride in their performance and expect to do better in the future. (Praise performance not achievements.)

8. Help them accept compliments graciously.

If we truly expect others in our environment to become

more effective and efficient in their responsibilities, we will encourage and build sound self-esteem — not only in others but also in ourselves.

Now that we know the things that are conducive to sound self-esteem let us take a look at eight things that perpetuate low self-esteem:

1. A people pleaser (trying so hard to please others that we make ourself and them miserable).

2. Working at a job that I don't like — one that is not fulfilling.

3. Destructive, devaluative, demeaning, self criticism.

4. Depending on others for my self worth (waiting for compliments from others).

5. Not allowing myself to achieve my full potential.

6. Giving up before I complete my goals.

7. Not speaking up for my convictions.

8. Feeling ignored or belittled (no one can belittle us without our permission).

If we were to summarize all the things that we do to lower our own self-esteem, we could probably put them under two major headings.

1. Our willingness to entrust the accountability for our own lives to other people.

2. Our tendency to confuse "what we are" with "how we act."

High self-esteem results primarily from our accepting complete responsibility for our own individual well being, and taking charge of our own lives. Be kind and considerate to yourself and allow yourself and others the right to make and profit from mistakes.

Accountability means *I make me* so let's examine some techniques for being accountable, for raising our own self-esteem, and also some suggestions for building sound self-esteem in our employees.

Suggestions:

1. Help them to see that they are beautiful and unique just the way they are.

2. Help them to understand that they need only compare with their own best self; don't compare self with others.

3. Help them to understand that they are not their actions. They are far more than their actions. If they fail in a project, it does not mean that they are failures.

4. Include more experiences that build self-reliance and accountability. Give them choices, alternatives. Allow them to see the consequences and pay value of their choices.

5. Point out to them how mistakes are stepping stones to achievement.

Some examples: Lou Brock, a baseball player, at age 35 set a world's record for stolen bases in one season. During that same season he was thrown out more times than 90 per cent of the players even tried to steal. He also held the record for the most times thrown out.

Thomas Edison made 10,000 mistakes on his way to inventing the light bulb. Thomas Edison had a saying, "When down in the mouth remember Jonah. He came out all right."

Babe Ruth for many years held the world's record for the number of home runs. He also held the world's record for strike outs. He struck out twice as many times as he hit home runs. He still holds the record for the number of home runs compared with the number of times he was at bat, one for 11. How many of us are willing to put it on the line 11 times for one success? Mistakes provide data needed to improve performance.

6. Share with them the beauty of enjoying each day one day at a time. How fortunate for each of us to have awakened this morning. The alternative is a bummer. How very fortunate to have gotten out of bed this morning because the alternative to that is also a bummer.

7. Praise them for their efforts. Remember always praise the *effort* not the *achievement* because if you only praise the

achievement and they don't achieve they might see it as a put down. Remember — *praise pays.*

Praise is so important to building positive attitudes and sound self-esteem in our employees. Praise turns losers into winners. When people think they are doing a good job and are praised for it, they work better, are happier, and more efficient and effective.

Some points on praising:

1. Praise closer and closer to approximations of the desired end. Each time they come closer to living up to your expectations praise them.

2. Look for the good things to praise. We can goal set and affirm in this area. "I enjoy catching my employees doing something good." When praising it is advisable to avoid "you" phrases; it is much better to use "I." Example: rather than saying: "You did a very good job on that project," say: "I sure like the effort that you put into that project. It was great."

3. When in doubt *praise!*

Don't depend on others to praise you. It is more common for people to find fault because they suffer from low self-esteem.

Let's now investigate ways for becoming accountable for raising our own self-esteem.

1. Lock out the negative destructive criticism that others might give of my performance. Have a purposeful *scotoma.* Just refuse to hear the garbage in. I am a positive person. I am not affected by the negative attitudes and opinions of others.

2. Control my self-talk. That conversation I have with myself about everything: *I always do that. Why am I so stupid? There I go again.*

My self-talk is three dimensional. *Words* trigger *pictures* and bring about *feelings.*

Much of my self-image and self-esteem is controlled by my own self-talk.

1. Start with performance
2. Mental evaluation or self-talk
3. Subconscious records it (truth, image)
4. Future performance affected.

The traditional limiting cycle controlling self-esteem is shown in the following illustration:

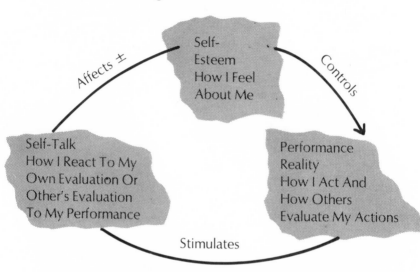

Performance stimulates my self-talk in either positive or negative ways. My self-talk affects me either positively or negatively. My self-esteem controls my performance. The higher my self-esteem the higher my performance. The one element that we have total control of is our self-talk. My greatest power is my power of choice. If I have the power to choose, I have the power to choose whether I am going to think or not to think. If I choose to think I can choose to think what I want to think. That's all that self-talk is.

My subconscious does not distinguish between a real experience and one that is vividly imagined with feelings. My self-talk triggers additional images or pictures that are recorded in my subconscious as wins or losses.

I make a public speech; 99 per cent of the speech is good. I make one small mistake. I evaluate and relive the mistake 20 times. "How could I be so stupid? I always blow it when I make a speech. I am lousy in front of a group." Words, pictures, feeling — my subconscious records 21 bad speeches.

My self-talk makes the difference between winning and losing, success or failure. It's a self-fulfilling prophecy. It's a sure-enough principle: "Every time I have to make a speech I blow it." Sure-enough.

To break the negative self-talk cycle we use the mini-cycle illustrated next:

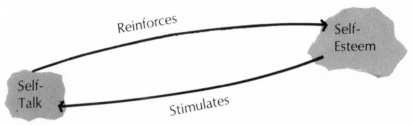

We can't always control our performance but we can control our self-talk thereby controlling our self-esteem. If we take accountability for controlling our self-talk then we become accountable for raising our own self-esteem. My performance will eventually rise to meet my self-esteem. Remember, I move toward and become like that which I think about all the time. Therefore, I want to become accountable for what I say to myself and what I think about.

1. Eliminate random negative affirmations that inflict guilt and lower self-esteem. (If I perform below my expectations or if I anticipate a poor performance I want to eliminate reinforcing it with negative self-talk.)

The following phrases need to be eliminated from your vocabulary:
• This is going to be tough
• I don't think I can do it

- There I go again
- What's the matter with me
- How could I be so stupid
- If only I would have
- I could have
- I should have
- Why am I not as good as so and so
- Why do I always
- I can't do anything right
- It happens every time
- It's going to be one of those days

If you will go over the preceding statements and substitute you for I you'll see how detrimental they are to lowering their self-esteem.

2. When performance does not live up to expectations instead of perpetuating poor performance with a demeaning negation, I silently affirm to myself:

That's not like me; next time I'll —

(Trigger the picture of the desired performance.) On good performances I will silently affirm to myself:

That's like me.

If you want to affirm for someone else simply add the word *you* for *me.*

We can begin to add rocks to the positive side of someone else's balance scale. Pretty soon they begin to counter old negative habits and attitudes. We need to be aware of the fact that some people have been accumulating rocks on the negative side for a long time. If they have accumulated 100 pounds of rocks on the negative side of their attitudinal balance scale, we are not going to make much of an impact by adding a few rocks. We must continue to add rocks to the positive side until we have put there more than a hundred pounds. When the attitudinal balance begins to move in the positive direction we still haven't gotten rid of those on the negative side; therefore, we need to continue to pile the rocks on the positive side.

Through awareness, accountability, and perseverance we can turn our bad performances into assets, and our good performances into powerful reinforcements for both ourselves and our employees.

Hostility: The constant companion of low self-esteem. No group or individual can survive with it. We build up a bank account of IOU's.

Several years ago, I was teaching a seminar to school district employees. One of the teachers who was attending decided to use the concepts being taught with her two teen-age daughters as well as with her students. Two weeks after the seminar we had a follow-up session. This teacher came to that session in tears. I encouraged her to stay afterwards. After the meeting she said that her family was worse than ever. She then began to explain the situation. She said that she went home and explained to her two daughters that from now on there would be no "have to's" in the family only "want to's." I asked her if she had talked about consequences. She said no, she had not. Well, it was easy to see what was going to happen. She explained that she and her husband had made plans to take the two girls out to dinner and as they were leaving the house the oldest daughter announced that she was not going. When asked why she replied: "I don't want to," so without the one daughter the family went out to eat dinner. Several days later the daughter asked her mother to drive her downtown so that she could go shopping. The mother replied, "No." The daughter asked her why? Whereupon the mother replied: "I don't want to." Needless to say the scene erupted into violence. The mother was being *hostile* toward the daughter. We display hostility in many different ways and they are all destructive.

I ordered a food processor for my wife for her birthday. It did not arrive in time for her birthday and my wife was disappointed. Several weeks later it arrived and they called my wife to tell her. My wife called me at the office and asked me to pick it up on my way home. When it was time to go home I got in my car, started the motor and set it on automatic pilot. I live 18 miles out of town and when I turned into my drive I remembered but it was too late because by the time I drove back to town the store would be closed. My wife was very disappointed because she planned to prepare dinner with it. I was embarrassed. I promised that I would bring it home the next day. The next day I once again neglected to bring it home. That evening when we went to bed my wife had a headache. That's known as:

1. **Withholding.**

We withhold our affection, our attention, our presence, our speech and our praises. Ways that we withhold:
- People who are habitually late.
- People who turn in reports late.
- People who never applaud.
- People who don't pay attention.
- People who talk when they need to listen.
- People who pout.

2. **Attacking on the subconscious level.**

Sarcasm, gossip, rumors, teasing, snide or cutting remarks.

3. **Entering territory boundaries.**

Leaving a mess in a shared office, squeezing toothpaste in the middle, leaving toothpaste cap off. Cutting grass but leaving uncut strip in the middle. Leaving tools out, not putting them back. Leaving dirty dishes for mom to find in morning.

The opposite of hostility is *warm regards*. That is the constant companion of high self-esteem, understanding, empathy, forgiveness, consideration, patience, support, love.

It is my choice:

I can live with and encourage hostility or. . .

I can live with and encourage warm regards for all people at all times.

I can overlook the bad qualities in others and choose to expand my self-image and lock on to the good qualities in others and reinforce the good. I can begin to catch them in the act of doing something right.

"I have warm positive regards for all people at all times." If we choose to make our environment one where people are supported and helped rather than one where they are criticized and put down, one might think about putting the following sign in many prominent places and talk about it:

PUT UP

OR

SHUT UP

In other words put someone up or don't say anything.

One might also encourage employees to put on a 3 x 5 inch index card:

I easily find ways to put myself and others up.

And

People feel best when they are around me.

Read this card several times a day and actually see yourself in the act of putting people up and how good that makes them feel. See people wanting to be around you because they know that you are going to make them feel good and how good that makes you feel.

You might discuss with colleagues the prospect of no put downs for any reason, not even for fun. If we slip we silently affirm: "That's not like me. Next time I will put myself and others up."

Effective Goal Setting Techniques

Before getting into specific details of goal setting, let's review some of the concepts that we have already covered and see how they fit into the over-all scheme of goal setting.

First, let's reexamine *accountability* (I make me). I take the responsibility for deciding what is of value and what's important to me. It means taking a look at how I got where I am. Have I made the choices based upon critical evaluation or have I allowed others to program me with *garbage?* How much of what I have stored in my subconscious is "truth?" How might I become more accountable for my own life? *Accountability is a way of life.* We want to become accountable for our own life and the direction we want to take; we do this by gaining control of our words, pictures, and feelings that we allow to become the "truth" about us.

Remember the sketch on the limiting cycle we referred to earlier, on controlling our self-esteem, that we show below.

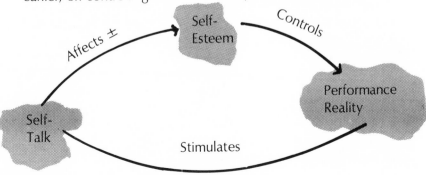

The cycle is a self-fulfilling prophecy. Our *performance* triggers *self-talk*, which raises or lowers our *self-esteem* and we can be accountable with the mini-cycle shown below:

We want to remember to:

1. Eliminate the negative devaluative statements about our performance and substitute: "That's not like me; next time I'll. . ." And on good performance: "That's like me."

2. We also want to become accountable for the *pictures* that are stored in our subconscious. We carry around a picture of where we are. In goal setting we want to begin to trigger pictures of where we want to be. The *I can be* zone. Unfortunately most of us have accepted the garbage in programming of others and that is what we have stored as "truth" and that is what controls our performance. We have all been conditioned to be where we are by others and our imagination takes over and it grows and grows. When the farmer plants a potato he doesn't get a bean. When the farmer plants a bean he doesn't get a bean. He gets many beans because between planting and harvest multiplication takes place. It's the same way with a thought. When you plant a negative thought you don't get a positive thought. When you plant a negative thought you don't get a negative thought, you get many negative thoughts. Between planting and harvest the imagination takes over and it grows and grows. But, hallelujah, turn that around. Plant a positive thought and you get many positive thoughts. Remember our imagination is not selective, is not discriminating, does not question. It simply accepts what is programmed. This is not necessarily what is best for us. If we continue to imagine ourself at a certain level we are not likely to change unless we be-

come accountable for the picture that we imagine for ourselves. Consistent imagination can thrust us up into the *I can be zone.*

Imagination x vividness = reality in my subconscious.

$$I \times V = RSC.$$

The subconsicous does not know the difference between a real experience and one that is vividly imagined, accompanied by feelings. By impressing clear and vivid pictures of what I truly want into my subconscious, I will begin to move toward those pictures very naturally.

We move toward and become like those things we think about all the time; therefore, if we continually dwell upon what we don't want that's what we get. Winners see what they want, losers see what they don't want.

3. We want to become accountable for our *feelings* also.

If I don't feel good about going to work on Mondays I probably won't do a good job.

If I don't feel capable about becoming an administrator, I will probably creatively avoid the opportunity when it presents itself.

Frequently, as administrators, we misuse our power, not intentionally, but because of a distorted awareness. Frequently, while dealing with people, we will catch them in the act of doing something wrong and continually point out all of the mistakes and expect them to take care of it.

What about all of the *good things* that this person does? Many people look up to you as a leader and when a leader takes time to recognize and praise the efforts of an activity one never forgets it.

Recognize how powerful you are in the eyes of your employees. Use that power with wisdom and forethought to really help employees to grow and become all that they are capable of becoming.

Do you recall earlier, when you saw the card with "fly," you had a challenging time to see the fly because you had locked on to the *black* on white. Again ask yourself, *"What am I locked on to in life?"*

What attitudes and opinions am I currently holding about myself, my colleagues, my employees, my institution, my job? Am I willing to grow with the changes required in my vocation, in my position?

Am I open to initiate more participatory management? Am I willing to move from demagogue to participatory manager?

Am I willing to get involved with employees in the solving of problems. Is my picture too limited, too restricted? *Remember:* We tend to gather data to support our old opinions and beliefs. We are perhaps more rationalizing than rational. Once we are "locked on" to something, we tend to "lock out" new opportunities, answers and solutions for our lives.

If there is one word that we want to lock out of our goal setting activities, it is *fear*.

Fear is the mainspring for restrictive motivation, fear of failure, rejection, ridicule, embarrassment, or punishment. . . But most of all, we are bothered by fear of the unknown.

Fear of the unknown is a great demotivator. It is perhaps the greatest single reason why more people are content looking into the past than into the future. We move toward and become like those things we think about. Therefore, if we dwell on the past we can't possibly grow.

Plutarch described the journey through life this way: *"We are like fearful water men, rowing our life boats with our back to the future, and our eyes on the past. . . How much greater we would be if we set our course by where we were going, rather than where we have been."*

There is a legend of two Arab tribes who were at war with one another. The leader of one of the tribes left instructions that all prisoners of war were to be brought to him before being executed. When the prisoners were brought before the leader he made them this proposition. At the far end of the room were two doors, a white door and a black door. The leader explained to the prisoners that they could choose either the white door or the black door. He further advised that on the other side of the white door was a firing squad. If they walked through the white door 10 guns were aimed at their heart and soldiers would all pull the trigger the moment they stepped through the white door. He also advised that if they wished they could take their chances and choose the black door. No one chose the black door. And on the other side of the black door was freedom. Rather than choose the unknown they chose death. The point is goal setting offers freedom, adventure, growth and satisfaction — if we step out of the shadow of fearing the future.

If we were to examine the ground to air missile we would find that it had several mechanisms built into it that caused the missile to behave in a certain way. When the missile is fired there is a homing mechanism that causes the missile to home in on some particular quality of the target — heat, magnetic, radar or infrared. Regardless of what atmospheric conditions cause the missile to veer off course, it is continuously making adjustments to get back on course. It also has another mechanism which causes it to self-destruct if there is no target (rather than come back down and kill innocent people). There is yet a third mechanism in the missile. When the missile makes contact with the target it self-destructs. Human beings are much like the missile. We are goal oriented beings. We are always making adjustments to get back on course. That's why it is so important to understand the rules of goal setting. We might be setting subconscious goals that cause us to self-destruct. Like the missile, we will self-destruct if we have no goals. We also will self-destruct when we make contact with our goal. You might think that whatever you do you are on a course of self-destruction. If you don't understand and observe the rules of goal setting this might very well be true.

We move toward that which we think about. That's why we want to be very selective in what we dwell on. We want to select carefully our *words, pictures* and *feelings.* This has to do with accountability. Don't let other people think for us. Don't demean ourselves with our own self-talk. Carefully select new goals and pictures to think about. The power of goal setting comes from giving our subconscious positive conflicts to deal with. Any thought held in our minds continuously must eventually be acted upon and become a reality. To quote Paul J. Meyer: "Whatever you vividly imagine, ardently desire, sincerely believe and enthusiastically act upon. . . must inevitably come to pass!" If I can hold to a clear, vivid picture of my goal, my creative subconscious will create the ways and means to get me there.

Successful people imagine their goals *way out* in front of them. They see clearly and vividly pictures of the end results. Lock onto these pictures. Trust your creative drive to bring these pictures to completion. This is how it works:

1. I have subconscious pictures of the kind of environment I like. This is known as my environmental self-image. People, home, recreation, job, etc.

2. These pictures are my expectations of reality.

3. The job of my creative subconscious is to maintain my reality, so. . .

4. . . . If I am above or below my expectations, dissonance occurs, and the creative subconscious either pushes me back, or drives me forward.

Perhaps the most important principle in goal setting is that *an individual team or group seldom exceeds its own expectations.*

(Even if the opportunity arises, we generally fail to capitalize on it.) The reason for this is our creative subconscious seeks to *maintain not surpass* our reality (expectations). A good example of this occurred several years ago.

I enjoy watching professional football on television. The Washington Redskins were a very exciting football team to watch. Then, they were composed mostly of cast offs. They called themselves, "the over the hill gang." But they always managed to win. They usually came from behind to do it. A friend of mine was playing for the Redskins at that time and I asked him: "Jeff, you guys were terrific. I could hardly wait to watch you on television. But you know you were rotten in the Super Bowl. Did you meet to find out what was wrong?" Jeff told me that they met for several days after the game. I asked Jeff what had been concluded. Jeff said they had concluded that they were the best prepared team ever to go to the Super Bowl. My response was: "How can you say that when you looked so bad?" Jeff said: "You know George Allen (coach) is a master psychologist. He painted on the ceiling Super Bowl. He purchased a red carpet with white lettering that read Super Bowl. Our knives, forks, spoons, plates, saucers, cups, had Super Bowl printed on them. Everything we touched had Super Bowl printed on it."

The Redskins had set a goal to go to the Super Bowl. They made contact with their goal and they self-destructed. They had lived up to their expectations. They should have set a goal to win the Super Bowl, not to get there.

Administrators will frequently goal set to get their first job and run into the doldrums soon after. They got what they were after but forgot to set a goal to be exciting and dynamic in their job. Or they goal set to use these concepts on the job but not at home. We goal set to drive home from vacation. When we drive in the driveway and walk in the door we collapse and sleep in our clothes. But if we had lived 100 miles further we would have made it and been just as tired. That's why it's so important to set big goals. Set goals far out in front. Remember: seldom do we exceed our own expectations.

To grow and change, I want to first change (raise) what I expect of myself on the subconscious level.

I want to clearly and vividly:
- See myself at a new income level.
- See myself in a new car.

- See myself enjoying that new home.
- See myself as a more *patient* and *dynamic* administrator.
- See myself as an empathic listener.
- See myself as creative.
- See myself as a leader.

$$\text{Imagination} \times \text{Vividness} = \text{Reality In My Subconscious}$$
$$I \times V = RSC$$

The clearer and more vividly I can imagine my new environmental self-image, the stronger will be the creative entry to attain these new expectations.

It sounds like such a simple principle, but not many people really understand or appreciate the power of goal setting.

A survey published several years ago pointed out that of people in the United States:

- 37 per cent hardly had any goals at all.
- 50 per cent have short-range goals only.
- 10 per cent have strong goals committed to memory.
- 3 per cent write their goals.

That 3 per cent rule the country.

Without goals we randomly move through life leaving great accomplishments to chance. Many of us are like a ball in a pinball machine, or a leaf in a windstorm.

Geese fly south in the winter not because they want to fly south but because they have to fly south. Squirrels gather nuts in the fall not because they want to but rather because they have to. Go out to the lake and watch the sailboats. Even though the wind is blowing in only one direction the sailboats are going in 360 different directions. The difference is there is a human at the helm. It's not the gale but the set of the sail that determines the direction you go.

Have you ever sat on the seat of a bicycle and without touching your feet to the ground try to maintain your balance. It's very difficult. But give that bicycle a direction and put it in motion and the balance factor disappears. The same is true with a life. A life standing still is very difficult to balance. But give that life direction and put it into motion and the balance factor disappears. This is what goals do. They give us a direction and put us in motion.

The most commonly ordered item in a restaurant is a "me too." We go into a restaurant not knowing what we want and someone orders a hamburger, french fries and a coke and four people respond, "Me too, me too, me too, me too." It's the same way in life. If we don't know what we want and some one makes a suggestion, we perform a "me too." We allow other people to set goals for us and we end up wondering what happened.

Let's summarize why goal setting is so important:

1. Setting goals gets information to our subconscious *right now*.

2. If it's on paper, we commit it to subconscious *indelibly*.

3. The creative subconscious automatically works to bring vividly imagined goals (pictures) to their attainment.

4. Goal setting automatically opens the reticular activating system to let through sensory messages important to the attainment of the goal.

5. Goals reduce or eliminate push/push back (provide inner direction instead of outer coercion).

6. Goals give us great energy and drive.

7. Goal setters procrastinate less (goal setters are action oriented).

8. Goals give us direction (the shortest distance between two points is a straight line).

9. Goal setters deal effectively with set-backs.

Several years ago I read an article about a young man named John Goddard. The article pointed out that when John was 15 years old he sat down and wrote down everything he ever wanted to do. Now for a 15 year old to sit down and dream is not too unusual but for a 15 year old to sit down and *write down* his dreams is a phenomenon. But that's what he did and that's what makes the difference. It's not enough to think 'em; you gotta ink 'em and think 'em. When one gets into the habit of inking 'em and thinking 'em we soon eliminate the "stinking thinking" and we all have an abundance of that to eliminate.

Never judge your goals. Never ask: "Am I big enough, small enough, rich enough, poor enough, smart enough, dumb enough?" Never ask *how*. The only questions to be asked when goal setting are: "What do I want and why do I want it?" The people who ask how, never set goals. They figure if they don't know how they shouldn't set the goal. If you knew how there would be no need for setting the goal. Just do it. Set the goal first and the how to's will come.

Some of the items on John Goddard's list were:

Type 50 w.p.m.

Visit movie studio.

Hold breath 2½ minutes under water.

Become an eagle scout.

Milk a rattle snake.

Read entire Encyclopedia Britannica.

Visit every country in the world.

Learn to speak French and Spanish.

Fly to the moon.

When that article was published he had just returned from a trip around the world scratching three more countries off of his list; he next scratched two more goals off of his list, raising his total to 97. Only 30 more to go. The key: he wrote his goals down. John Goddard said: "I'll bet there aren't 100 people in the world who write down their desires without telling themselves at the same time that it can't be done." The thing that makes John Goddard unique is life-time goals based on his fondest dreams.

Why don't all of us set goals for the things we really want out of life?

We look at things objectively, logically, intellectually, and it

doesn't make sense.
1. No one has ever done it before.
2. I have never done it before.
3. Statistics show that _____.
4. We don't think that we are worthy of it.
5. I don't deserve _____.
6. Things like that are for others.
You can eventually have anything you want. If you
- Clearly see it.
- Lock onto the picture.
- Lock out the I can'ts, I musn'ts, I have to's.
- Have faith in your creative mechanisms.

"Whatever the mind can conceive and believe it can achieve." What follows is a most profound lesson in goal setting. Draw on a piece of paper 9 dots as they appear below.

These are the instructions for the nine dot puzzle*

With four straight lines connect all nine dots without retracing; without picking your pen or pencil from the paper.

When goal setting we want to remember not to place limitations on ourself. We want to get outside our nine dots. Most people attempt to solve the problem by staying inside the nine dots or without crossing the line. Neither one of these restrictions were imposed. But we imposed them on ourself.

How many arbitrary limitations do we impose on ourself in life? How many times do we say: "That's not for me — I could never have something that good or that big?"

How many of us quit dreaming of adventure before we even get out of college?

*Solution on page 112

Why quit dreaming?

Why limit ourselves in life?

How many administrators do you know who died at the age of 35 and were not buried until age 65? How many administrators do you know who have retired but have failed to notify the board?

So many people think that setting your goals too high and missing is the problem. That's not the problem. The problem is setting your goals too low and hitting. Set big goals. Even if you miss you are better for having tried. I would much rather attempt to do something great and fail than attempt to do nothing and succeed. I would much rather aim at a star and hit an eagle than aim at an eagle and hit a rock. All of us want to leave footprints on the sands of time, but we can't do it sitting on our butts. And who wants to leave buttprints on the sands of time.

1. Billie Jean King

   A young child of 5'1", 100 pounds overweight, thick glasses, wrote her dream! *To be a world renowned tennis champ.*

2. Jean Claude Killy

   At thirteen years old, wrote his dream on an envelope: *To win three gold medals in skiing.*

3. James Irwin dreamed of being an astronaut; but in 1960 was in a plane crash. Broke both legs and his jaw, which had to be wired. He lost his memory and underwent psychotherapy. He applied *four times* for the Corps of Astronauts and was refused. He became the eighth man to walk on the moon.

Allow yourself to dream. Billie Jean King did; Jean Claude Killy did; James Irwin did.

Let's now investigate the *rules of goal setting.*

1. Balance your goals (the big picture).

Figure out the "star graph" of your life and set goals in all areas

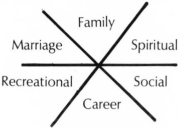

I have a friend that used to be a public educator. There were things that he wanted to do with and for his family that he could not afford to do as a public educator. He went into sales. After a brief period of time he saw an opportunity to become national sales manager. Using the very concepts that we are sharing with you, he became national sales manager. One night sitting on the edge of his hotel bed in New York, he was thinking: "Boy oh boy, now I'll be able to do all of those things that I have wanted to do with and for my family." And then he thought: "My family!" He had not seen his family in 63 days. He had no social life, no recreational life, no spiritual life. He was totally destroying himself for the sake of one goal. His star graph would have looked like the following:

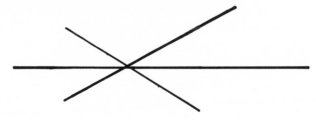

It would have been unbalanced. If one would put a rim around the first sketch and roll it down the street one would have a relatively smooth ride. But if one would put a rim

around the second and roll it down the street one would have a very rough ride.

Unfortunately, that is precisely what many of us do. My wife did this in the family. She goal set so hard with the children that she ceased to be a person.

We have all known people who excelled in one or two areas of life, but who had not bothered to develop themselves in other areas. If I use all of my energy and creativity in one or two areas, I am destined to mediocrity in others.

2. Set priorities; be consistent.

I want to set priorities. I ask myself what are the things that I value most in my life in order of priorities. By doing this I accomplish two things. I am able to determine my values and I have decided what's most important. I should then set a goal in my first priority. Every goal that I set in every other area of my life should support the achievement of that goal. A person or group is no more stable than their uppermost goal in life. Make sure it's a very stable goal.

1 2 3 4

All my goals are heading in the same direction. I have a friend who attended one of my seminars. Six months later he called and said: "Steve, I am losing my family." I suggested that we have lunch, which we did, and I asked him to explain. He said when I had talked about setting *quality* tirne goals with my family that he had never heard of anything like that. His father had always been a busy man and spent little time with the family. Consequently he really didn't know how to spend quality time with his family. He decided that he was going to purchase a 40-foot sailboat. He couldn't afford the sailboat so he got a second job in order to earn enough money to pay for it. He was seeing his family less and doing poor work on both jobs. His goals were not consistent. They were pulling him in many different directions.

Consistency and compatibility are very important to group goal setting. It is important that the individual's goals are in line and headed in the same direction as the team goals. If you were to take a bar of iron and examine the qualities you would find that it had many. You would find that it was composed of billions of molecules. These molecules are in constant motion in all directions. If you would take a wire and coil it around the bar of iron and subject it to an electrical current, you would find that the molecules are still in constant motion but now they are all in motion in the same direction. One hasn't diminished any of the original qualities but one has created one more. It has become a magnet and magnets are attracted to things. The same is true with life. If all of our goals are headed in the same direction we are attracted to life. And waking up is the most important part of the day.

3. Make your goals constructive and positive.

If I have a bad temper I don't set a goal not to have a bad temper. That's what I don't want. I set a goal to be calm, cool, and collected. That's what I do want. If I decide to set some health goals and I decide I want to weigh 160 pounds, I don't set a goal to lose 30 pounds. That's what I don't want. I set a goal to weigh 160 pounds. That's what I do want. I must be able to visualize my goal. I can't visualize losing 30 pounds but I can visualize myself weighing 160 pounds. I don't want to set a goal not to be a demagogue but rather to be a participatory manager. One wants to motivate oneself constructively and see the *pay value, personal profitability;* not restrictively (fear).

4. Set goals that are clearly defined and specific.

We are frequently called in to be a goal consultant for both individuals and corporations. The first thing I ask clients is: "Do you have them *written down?*" If the answer is "no," I tell them I can't help them. If the answer is "yes," then the very first thing we investigate is if they are clearly defined and specific. This, next to writing them down, is probably the most important rule of goal setting.

Occasionally my wife will say: "Honey, I'm going shopping." When she says that I know that she is going to be gone several hours and she will probably come back with nothing. However, if she says: "Honey, I'm going grocery shopping," I know then that she will be gone a couple of hours and she will come back with a station wagon full of groceries. She is clear and specific.

You wouldn't walk up to a clerk in the grocery store and ask: "Give me some groceries." They would look at you as if you were nuts. You would have a grocery list and with a shopping cart you would check off the things that you put in the cart. You would not walk into a restaurant and ask the waitress for some food. No, you first want a menu and from the menu you would make your selection, or perhaps you would order a "me too." You would never set a goal to be a good administrator or a good husband or a good father. No. You would decide what does it mean to be a good administrator, husband or father. What does it look like? You would then set your goals accordingly. You would be clearly defined and specific. The same is true in the story that I related earlier, about the Washington Redskins. They set a goal to get to the Super Bowl. They should have set a goal to win the Super Bowl.

The clearer the picture the faster we arrive because the reticular activating system knows what to look for.

5. Lock on to the end result and all of its parts.

That's what motivates us: *the end result.* People will ask me: "Steve, what motivates you?" I'm appalled by this question. The end result is what motivates me. What else could possibly motivate .one? Surely it's not the day-to-day chores. It's hard for me to get motivated to fill out forms or make phone calls for appointments. It's the closing of the sale, the receiving that grant, having that loving relationship, etc. If goals are clearly defined we don't have to know all of the steps involved to get there. One does not need to be a walking encyclopedia. See the end result and have faith (belief without evidence) that your creative subconscious will take care of the sub goals along the way.

A goal is a positive conflict to your creative subconscious, and it will resolve the conflict if you just hold on to the picture.

Rules three, four and five are all involved with opening the reticular activating system. Know what you want; vividly see it in your mind; lock on to the end result and your filter system will be wide open to the relevant information.

You may hear people say, "My goal is to be happy." "My goal is to be successful."

Unless you *know exactly* what happiness is and what it takes to make you happy or successful, these goals will probably never be realized. The reticular activating system does not know what to be open to.

6. Lock out time restrictions.

Some goals automatically have time restrictions and there is nothing that one can do about that.

Examples: Bills, attending scheduled events.

Time restrictions are not necessarily good for goal setting because: they put us out of our comfort zone. Make us press if too short or procrastinate if too long. Have you ever noticed how busy you get on March 21 if you have a project due on March 22? The busiest day of the year for the United States

Postal Service is April 15. We keep procrastinating and end up spending all night filling out our income tax return.

It causes us to have limited awareness and we develop scotomas to short cuts and solutions. The way to beat time restrictions is to see the end result as if it had already been achieved. The above mentioned is in reference to *long range goals.*

7. Keep your goals to yourself, share them only with those who can help you achieve them.

When I was a child I was brought up during the Depression, which meant we had very little of anything including food. Whatever we ate, we either grew it, caught it, or shot it. That's how we fed ourselves. We lived close to where the salt water and fresh water mixed. That's a good place to go crabbing. One day my mother told us to go catch some crabs because she wanted to fix some for supper. Now we knew what that meant. There were no freezers so we didn't have frozen food, very few canned goods. So when mom said she wanted to have crab for supper we knew that if we didn't catch any crab we would not have any supper. We lived about three miles from where the salt water and fresh water mixed. We got there at a perfect time of the tide. When we arrived we discovered that we had neglected to bring something to put the crabs in after we caught them. Now if you have ever held a live crab in your hand you know that you give them your undivided attention. You don't hold a crab in one hand and fish for others with the other hand. We didn't have time to go back home and get something because we would lose the tide. One of the kids suggested that we dig a hole and put them in it. We did and we went out to get some crabs. As we caught them we went and put them in the hole. When we were through we found that none of the crabs had escaped. Every time one would try to crawl out of the hole the others would reach up and pull him back into the hole. They would not let one another escape.

That's what people will do to you. They will sabotage your goals. They will give you a thousand reasons why you can't do that. Now I didn't say: "Don't share your goals." I said: "Share them only with those who can help you reach them." If, for example, there is a position available that you are qualified for and want, then you certainly want to let the person or persons know that you are interested in that position.

Another reason that one does not want to share his goals is that it dissipates creative energy. Talking about it is almost like accomplishing it, so positive tension seems to diminish. It's like a balloon full of air (energy). Let go of the balloon and what happens? It flutters all over the place and falls to the floor limp and lifeless. That's what happens when we share our goals.

8. Reset your goals as you approach them (update).

This is how one keeps from self-destructing. If we make contact with our goals, just like the missile, we self-destruct. I want to set my goals just as high as I can honestly and clearly see. Start just as high as I can see myself right now. When I ap-. proach my original goal and can see myself beyond, *then reset* my goals.

9. Write them down.

Writing down goals takes them out of the realm of chance. When we write them down we use three out of the five modes of perception. We *see* them, we *touch* them and when we read them we *hear* them. It makes an indelible imprint in my subconscious.

Now ask yourself: What are the five things you value most in life in order of priorities?

Action Plan

Do it! Do it right! Do it right now!

Once you have done this, take out five blank sheets of paper. At the top of each paper put down one of the five things that you value most. On each of those blank pages write down all of the things that you would like to accomplish.

For example:

Self	Family
Spiritual	Wife
Health	Children
Physical	Brothers
Weight	Sisters
Emotional, etc.	Mom and Dad

Mankind	Country

In other words if self is my number one priority I would write self at the top of one sheet. Then I would divide that into spiritual, health (physical, emotional). What are some things that I would want to accomplish under physical health? Weight 178 pounds; blood pressure 120/68; cholesterol under 200; triglycerides under 100, etc. I do that for each priority. Once I have completed the five sheets I then go back to each sheet and decide which three would I like to most accomplish *under each* priority and I put an A by the three that I would most like to accomplish in each priority. I then go back to each sheet and decide which one I would like to do most. Second most and third most in each priority and put a 1, 2, and 3 behind the A. I will end up with A1, A2 and A3 under each priority. You now have what you might call a *dream list*. This is the list from which you set your goals. Remember: take off the judge's robe and your conditioned expectations. Regardless of how wild or far out an idea might seem — if you think of it put it down. One wants to update one's *dream* list twice a month. So place it where you will be reminded to do so.

What we are discussing here is changing attitudes and attitudes are formed by three-dimensional self-talk — words which trigger pictures which bring about feelings. We are now going to discuss how you can become accountable for your own self-talk, thus your own attitudes.

Remember my analogy about a glass full of water? If I had a glass filled to the rim with water and I also had a pile of rocks and I dropped a rock into the glass of water, the water would be displaced by the weight of the rock. If I continued to do this I would continue to displace the water. I would never get rid of all of the water but I would eventually end up with more rocks than water. The same is true when we are working with attitudes. We don't erase the old attitude but rather we create a new dominant reality.

The same is true if we had a playground see-saw and on one edge we had a hundred pounds of rocks. If we began putting rocks on the opposite edge we would need to put more than one hundred pounds before it began to move in the opposite direction. But we would not have gotten rid of the rocks on the other edge. That's why when we get it moving in our chosen direction we can't stop. Because, someone might dump a load of garbage on the other edge.

The rocks that we have referred to are words. The way that we will become accountable for the words is through the constructive use of affirmative reminders. That in turn will trigger the pictures in our imagination we want rather than pictures we don't want. We then begin to form new H.A.B.A.T.T. (Have A Ball All The Time. Happy And Beautiful All The Time) patterns. As long as we are forming new habit patterns we might as well form those that cause us to feel happy and beautiful all the time. By becoming accountable we then begin to get the correct operating thoughts into our subconscious so that we can become the person that we are capable of becoming.

An affirmative reminder is a statement of fact or belief about a reality as I perceive it. I have made them all of my life and will continue to do so. They have pretty much shaped my self-image and self-esteem. It's exciting to become aware to such an extent that I now understand that I can become accountable for the affirmative reminders that I make and thus for my self-image and self-esteem. How does one properly structure an affirmation?

I see myself as if the desired goal or change has already taken place. Now I describe myself and how I feel.

Rules for structuring a proper affirmation.

1. It needs to be personal. It begins with "I. "

2. It needs to be positive. It says what I want, not what I don't want.

3. It needs to be present tense. Will, going to and can are no-no's. We are programming the subconscious; and the subconscious can only be programmed in present tense.

4. It needs to include action and excitement words as much as possible.

Through continuous repetition of affirmative reminders we revise the data in our subconscious. The new "truth" conflicts with the old "reality." Our creative subconscious makes sure we act according to the currently dominant image of "reality" in our subconscious. It's the cognitive dissonance theory that we related in an earlier chapter. I accomplish four things by using affirmative reminders.

1. I revise the "truth" in my subconscious. I create a new dominant "reality" and I must act like that reality.

2. I build new and powerful habit patterns, habits of thought and habits of action.

3. My creative subconscious automatically and continually sends me the data needed to reach my goal. This is the reticular activating system that was explained earlier in this book.

4. My creative subconscious automatically provides the energy, creativity and motivation needed. That's why it is so very important to set high goals, to make certain that we are provided with enough energy, creativity and motivation.

What we need to do at this time is guide you through a plan of action for goal setting.

1. List your goals. What do you want?

Expanded outpatient health services. Health promotion programs. Help people with sane living habits. Nonsmoking clinics, obesity clinics, healthful eating clinics.

2. Why do I want to do this? What is the pay value?

Personal satisfaction, help people feel well. Help people to achieve their health goals, help people to become more fulfilled.

3. What are the obstacles and road blocks? Why haven't you reached your goals before?

No public awareness, was not thought to be our role, no funds allocated, no demand.

4. What are some possible solutions to the obstacles? What needs to be done?

Conduct an awareness campaign describing the needs. Convince the board of the needs for this service. Set aside money for next year's budget. Conduct an advertising and promotion campaign.

5. Your goal affirmation (I see myself as if the goal or change has already taken place. Now I describe myself and how I feel. Personal, positive, present tense.)

I am very pleased and fulfilled administering, as part of our total program, a program that is helping well people stay well and providing them with data to assist them in living long healthy lives.

6. Supportive affirmations. All of the information in No. 4 wants to be included in these supportive affirmations.

I enjoy convincing our board of the needs for a wellness program. It is exciting to spearhead a campaign toward public awareness of the need for a wellness program. I am pleased that our board has approved the budgeting of money for this program.

Let's go through the same six steps in planning a personal goal:

1. Goal.

To weigh 168.

2. Pay value.

Personal satisfaction, better appearance, more energy, better health, more endurance.

3. Obstacles and road blocks.

Snacking between meals, portions too large, eating wrong kinds of foods, not exercising.

4. What are the solutions?

Eat up to three times a day, eat smaller portions, eat the proper kinds of food, begin a daily exercise program.

5. Goal affirmation.

I feel super slim, trim and healthy in my new clothes now that I weigh 168. I feel great at 168.

6. Supportive affirmations.

I eat only at regularly scheduled meal times.

I enjoy filling up on smaller portions of the proper kinds of foods.

I am exhilarated doing my daily exercise schedule of walking, jogging, bike riding and weight lifting.

Now take a 3 x 5 index card and transfer the above data onto it. On one side put down the goal (no. 1) and underneath it put down pay value (no. 2). On the other side of the card put down no. 5 — the goal affirmation. Underneath the goal put down the supportive affirmations (no. 6).

Example:

Side No. 1

1.	Goal: More compassionate spouse and parent
2.	Pay value: Happier environment Peace in home Love in home Harmony in home Healthier

Side No. 2

5. | I am a super compassionate husband and father who shows God is alive to his family.

6. | I know my family better and enjoy them more now that my time with them is undivided. I look forward anxiously and selfishly to our time together.

How to use your affirmation card:

I would suggest that you carry your goal cards in your day-timer or wrap a rubber band around them and carry them in your shirt pocket or inside coat pocket. Carry them in a place so that you are reminded of them. I suggest that you read your cards a *minimum* of three times a day. Preferably when you arise in the morning before you get out of bed and again just before retiring in the evening and sometime in between. When you read the words vividly imagine yourself having already accomplished the affirmed statement. You then allow yourself to experience how you will feel when you have accomplished the goal.

AFFIRMATIONS FOR BUILDING SELF-ESTEEM*

1. I am a valuable and important person and I'm worthy of the respect of others.

2. I'm optimistic about life; I look forward to and enjoy new challenges to my awareness.

3. I am my own expert, and I allow others the same privilege.

United Learning Institute, Incorporated
*Copyright © 1973 By Lilburn S. Barksdale

4. I express my ideas easily, and I know others respect my point of view.

5. I am aware of my value system and confident of the decisions I make based on my current awareness.

6. I have a positive expectancy of reaching my goals, and I bounce back quickly from temporary setbacks.

7. I have pride in my past performance and a positive expectancy of the future.

8. I accept compliments easily and share my successes with others who have contributed to them.

9. I feel warm and loving toward myself, for I am a unique and precious being, ever doing the best my awareness permits, ever growing in wisdom and love.

10. I am actively in charge of my life and direct it in constructive channels. My primary responsibility is for my own growth and well being (the better I feel about myself, the more willing and able I am to help others).

11. I am my own authority (and I am not affected by negative opinions or attitudes of others).

12. It is not what happens to me, but how I handle it, that determines my emotional well being.

13. I'm a success to the degree that I feel warm and loving toward myself.

14. No one in the entire world is more or less worthy, more or less important, than I.

15. I count my blessings and rejoice in my growing awareness.

16. I am an action person; I do first things first and one thing at a time.

17. I am warm and friendly toward all I contact; I treat everyone with consideration and respect.

18. I am kind, compassionate and gentle with myself.

This procedure is not a new one. You have been affirming all of your life and you will continue to do so the rest of your life.

Our project is to deliberately control the input of information and thus direct the changes we intend to make in our performance.

Before discussing the rules for group goal setting let me mention a few observations that I think are necessary for group survival. I also believe that they are absolutely essential if we are going to grow and exist. These are necessary to establish before setting group goals. These may be applied to any group from a family to a large corporation or government.

I believe that the first thing that a group needs to do is to establish its purpose for existence. Once the purpose has been established it is then necessary to determine the various functions. Once the functions have been agreed upon, we begin to set goals to accomplish the functions.

Rules for group goal setting:
1. Balance your goals.
   Consider all of the functions of the group.
2. Be consistent and compatible.
   The more the group goals agree with the goals of the individuals within the group the more effective the group.
3. Be constructive and positive.

See what you want not what you don't want.
4. Clearly define and be specific.
Short range goals place a time limit. One might want to call these strategies. For the long range goals one does not want to set time limits.
5. Write them down (ink 'em and think 'em).
6. Collectively lock on to a picture of the end result, establish the pay value.
7. Share only with those who can assist you.
8. Update regularly.

Some challenges of group goal setting:
1. Being able to communicate the picture of the end result so that all can visualize it.
2. Being able to make a decision which is supported by *all*.
3. Working together in harmony.

A problem-solving model for individual or group use:
I. Where are you?
The objective is to create a description of "where you are" currently, which can be understood and accepted by different group members.
A. State the problem in general.
B. Brainstorm thoughts, ideas, facts and feelings which *explain the problem* (at this point one does not offer solutions; we are trying to explain the problem).
1. Invite input from all.
2. Avoid editing and discussing the input.
3. Make the input visible so that all can see (chalkboard, flip chart, butcher paper).
4. Some helpful questions for yourself and your group.
A. Who is affected?
B. Who is causing the problem?
C. What kind of problem is it?
• Is leadership lacking?

- Is there a lack of clarity about purpose, functions or goals?
  - Are norms too restrictive?
  D. Write a problem statement, a brief specific summary of the input that answers: Who is affected? Who is causing it? What kind of problem is it?

II. What is our intent?

The objective is to create a clear picture of where we want to be. The picture, when achieved, solves the problem.

  A. Brainstorm all possible *solutions* to the problem. No solution is too wild. We will not edit each others creativity.
  B. Make goal statements. Translate the solution(s) into specific goal(s). Descriptions of where we want to be.
  C. Rank in order the three or four goal statements which best solve the problem.
  D. Submit each of the goals to the force field analysis.

	Forces For	**Forces Against**
Goal _____ _____ _____ _____		
Goal _____ _____ _____ _____		
Goal _____ _____ _____ _____		

E. Decide: Consider the data of the force field and write the goal(s) which best solve(s) your problem.

III. Now do it.
The objective is to create a plan of action that is specific enough so the various people can agree about who is to do what and when.
A. Brainstorm actions the group might take to accomplish the decided upon goal(s).
    1. Be certain to respond to the data generated in the force field.
B. Decide on the most effective actions.
C. Action plan.
    1. What are the actions?
    2. Who is doing it?
    3. When will it be finished?

Actions:	Who:	When Action Is To Be Finished:

D. When do we meet to assess our progress?
There was this very poor family from Italy. The mother and father wanted to provide the children with opportunities that they never had. They decided that the best way to do this was to move to the United States of America. The father went out and found a second job and they saved every dime possible. Finally they had saved enough to purchase third class transportation on a steam ship.

Their friends and neighbors were saddened to see them leave but they were happy that they had reached their goal. They were also very poor but wanted to do something for them to show them how much they loved them. They decided to bake some bread and make some cheese and give it to them to eat on the trip across. As they were boarding the ship the friends and neighbors gave them the cheese and bread. The fifth day out the young 10 year old son told his father: "I can't stand the smell of that cheese and bread, it makes me sick just to look at it."

The father reached into his pocket and pulled out a quarter and told his son: "Maybe someone on this ship has an apple or banana that they will sell you."

The boy took the quarter and went up on deck. He was gone one hour and a half. Two hours. Two hours and a half. The father thought, he must be lost. The father went on the deck and began to search for his son. The father passed by two large glass doors and as he peered in he saw a large chandelier and a beautiful red carpet. He decided to go into the room to get a better look. As he entered this large banquet room and looked down to his left he saw his son sitting at a table with several different kinds of meats, vegetables, breads, drinks and deserts. The father was shocked and asked his son: "What are you doing?" Whereupon the son told his father he was eating.

The father said: "I know it but who is going to pay for it?"

The son told his father: "It was included in the price of the ticket."

Most of us go through life sitting in the hold of the ship eating cheese and bread, while all the while the banquet has been included in the price of the ticket.

Life is a banquet and most of us are starving to death. Go out and partake of it.

Remember: "People don't care how much you know, until they know how much you care."

Finally I would like to share with you the greatest one-liner

I've ever heard. Supposedly Henry Ford first said it. "Whether you think you can or whether you think you can't you're right."

Solution to puzzle on page 89

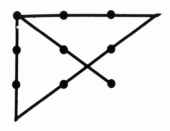

STEVE MUSSEAU is president of United Learning Institute, Inc., of Colorado. A nationally known speaker and motivator, Mr. Musseau is perhaps best known for presenting ULI's two-day seminar on Increasing Human Effectiveness. He has presented that seminar and related ULI programs to more than one million people working in a great variety of industries.

For 21 years Mr. Musseau applied his background of science, physical education and psychology teaching to motivating young people in all levels of education from elementary school through college. In addition, he successfully coached football at the high school, junior college and university levels. His teams won championships for eight of the fourteen years he served as a head coach. He was selected as a nominee for Coach of the Year by the American Football Coaches Association.

In 1974, Mr. Musseau began his full-time activities devoted to helping people understand personal and professional goal-setting concepts. He taught people how to apply various techniques which would help them help themselves to improve their lives. He has worked with children, teenagers, adults and family groups as well as local and national organizations.

In 1977 Mr. Musseau moved to Colorado Springs where he became president of ULI of Colorado. A family man (twelve children), he brings sensitivity and understanding to his topic. Mr. Musseau has a Bachelor of Science degree from Louisiana State University and over 100 hours of graduate studies.

United Learning Institute, Inc., established in 1974, has twelve offices in the United States. The institute offers many programs designed to help "build people". In addition to public seminars for individuals the institute has provided "people building" programs for over 240 organizations.

Notes

Notes

Notes